Selected Tables, Charts
and Formulas
for the
STUDENT
CINEMATOGRAPHER
from the
AMERICAN
CINEMATOGRAPHER
MANUAL

EDITED BY
Stephen H. Burum, ASC

THE ASC PRESS
HOLLYWOOD, CALIFORNIA

Selected Tables, Charts and Formulas
for the Student Cinematographer
from the American Cinematographer Manual

Revised Second Edition

ISBN 0-935578-35-8

Introduction

The *American Cinematographer Manual* is a professional resource that is used by cinematographers around the world. Conceived by Hollywood feature-film cinematographers over 75 years ago, the manual is designed to be a complete reference source on the set. It covers every aspect of cinematography from lens to lab. The current edition encompasses more than 880 pages.

Over the last decade, many schools and universities have introduced courses in filmmaking, and interest in the art and craft of cinematography has grown. We have endeavored to meet this burgeoning interest with this book, which was designed with a student budget in mind.

Selected Tables, Charts and Formulas for the Student Cinematographer comprises subjects from the *American Cinematographer Manual* that are most relevant and helpful to the student. This material reflects the basic concepts of our craft; these tables, charts and formulas are the same ones used by professionals. We have carefully chosen key areas that will enlighten and inform. Look closely over these pages, and you will find a great deal of useful information embedded in the charts and tables.

If you become obsessed with cinematography — and we hope you will — there is no better book in the world than the comprehensive *American Cinematographer Manual.* We also recommend *Charles Clarke's Professional Cinematography* and *Reflections: Twenty-One Cinematographers at Work* as cinematography textbooks. For current news you should subscribe to our monthly publication *American Cinematographer* magazine.

Board of Governors
American Society of Cinematographers

Table of Contents

Origins of The American Society of Cinematographers

Since 1919, the ASC has remained true to its ideals: loyalty, progress, artistry. Reverence for the past and a commitment to the future have made a potent and lasting combination in a world of shifting values and uncertain motives.

The American Society of Cinematographers received its charter from the State of California in January 1919 and is the oldest continuously operating motion picture society in the world. Its declared purpose still resonates today: "to advance the art of cinematography through artistry and technological progress, to exchange ideas and to cement a closer relationship among cinematographers."

The origins of the ASC lie in two clubs founded by cinematographers in 1913. The Cinema Camera Club was started in New York City by three cameramen from the Thomas A. Edison Studio: Phil Rosen, Frank Kugler and Lewis W. Physioc. They decided to form a fraternity to establish professional standards, encourage the manufacture of better equipment and seek recognition as creative artists. Meanwhile, the similarly conceived Static Club was formed in Los Angeles. When Rosen came to the West Coast five years later, he and Charles Rosher combined the clubs. The ASC now has more than 340 active and associate members.

The first ASC screen credit was given to charter member Joseph August when he photographed a William S. Hart picture in 1919.

The year after its charter, ASC began publishing *American Cinematographer* magazine, which ever since has served as the club's foremost means of advancing the art.

Currently our technology committee has created a standard test (StEM) for digital cinema. They are advising the industry on standards in both production and postproduction for digital capture, manipulation and presentation.

The ASC is not a labor union or guild, but is an educational, cultural and professional organization. Membership is possible by invitation and is extended only to directors of photography with distinguished credits in the industry.

— George E. Turner

Responsibilities of the Cinematographer

I. PreProduction

A. Conceptual Research and Design
- Discuss all aspects of script and director's approach to picture in preliminary talks with director
- Analyze script as whole
- Analyze story structure
- Analyze characters
- Research period, events, general subject and appropriate design elements
- Devise style, visualize approach
- Continue talks with director on new ideas
- Come to agreement with director
- Discuss and come to agreement with production designer
- Discuss and research with technical advisor

B. Practical Research and Design
- Ascertain or find out budget requirements
- Scout and approve locations
- Plot sun position for locations
- Check local weather
- Check tide tables near ocean
- Review, discuss and approve set plans
- Review, discuss and approve spotting plans for stages
- Review and approve props, picture cars, airplanes, boats, horse-drawn vehicles, mock-ups and miniatures

C. Technical Research and Design
- Visit laboratory to calibrate, customize and evaluate exposure system for any combination of electronic or chemical image capture; establish developing, printing, set timing and transfer protocols
- Visit equipment vendors
- Explore new equipment
- Learn how new equipment works
- Invent (or cause to be invented) special equipment or techniques for show
- Standardize and create effects bible for show
- Help create and approve any storyboards

- Design (or cause to be designed) and approve any built-in or practical lighting fixture
- Design lighting-plot plan and rigging for stages and locations with gaffer and key grip

D. Quality Control
- Choose and approve crew, film stock, lab, equipment, second-unit and visual-effects crews
- Supervise manufacture and testing of new or modified equipment
- Visit sets under construction
- Approve wild walls, ceiling pieces and any moving set pieces
- Check lighting-fixtures crew
- Walk locations and stages with all departments to discuss requirements
- Approve set colors and textures
- Approve costume colors and textures
- Approve make-up and hair
- Generate (or cause to be generated) and approve equipment lists for camera, electric and grip
- Check dailies screening rooms for correct standards

E. Implementation
- Cast stand-ins
- Train crew to use any new equipment
- Walk locations and stages with director and devise shooting plan
- Make list of special equipment for production manager and indicate number of days required
- Work with assistant director on shooting schedule (order of and days required for each scene)
- Estimate and order film stock (type, size, quantity)
- Generate (or cause to be generated) and approve rigging and shooting manpower and man-days
- Assist other departments in getting required equipment, manpower and tests.
- Drop by all departments and visit department heads at least twice a day to answer any questions
- Mediate any problems between departments
- Check loading of production trucks or cargo containers for location or international shipping
- Visit cast run-through and rehearsals
- Advise and back up director on any problems
- Help producer or studio solve any production problems

F. Testing
- Shoot tests for style
- Shoot tests for lab
- Shoot tests for lighting of principal actors
- Shoot tests for camera and lenses
- Shoot tests for wardrobe and makeup
- Shoot tests for any special effects processes, unusual rigs, props or methods

II. Shooting

A. Planning
- Check and approve all call sheets and shooting order of the day's work

B. Blocking
- Watch rehearsal of scene to be shot
- Devise shot list with director (coverage)
- Choose lens and composition, show to director for approval
- Make sure composition and movement fulfill scene task
- Work out mechanical problems with camera operator, assistant camera, dolly and crane grips
- Set any camera-movement cues
- Place stand-ins and rehearse, fine-tune
- Ensure proper coverage of scene for editor
- Work with assistant director on background action

C. Lighting
- Design lighting to show set/location to best advantage relative to story, style and dramatic content
- Light each actor to reinforce and reveal character
- Make sure mood and tone of light help tell story
- Design light for minimum reset time between set-ups
- Utilize stand-by painter for control of highlights, shadows, aging, dusting down of sets and props
- Set and match light value, volume, color and contrast of each setup (exposure)
- Set any lighting cues (dimmers, spot lights, color changes and any pre-programming)

D. Preparation
- Work out any sound problems
- Work out any problems with other departments
- Check, set and approve all stunts with stunt coordinator
- Set any additional cameras required for stunts

- Double-check safety with all concerned
- Show shot to director to make any final changes
- Get actors in for final mechanical rehearsal; solve any outstanding problems

E. Photography
- Photograph scene
- Approve or correct take
- Check parameters and reset for next take
- Shoot any plates
- Shoot any video playback material
- Move to next setup

F. Administrative
- Define first setup in morning and after lunch
- Make sure stills are taken of scene
- See that "making of" and/or EPK crews get needed footage
- Make sure script supervisor has any special camera or lighting notes
- Check film raw stock inventory
- Try to shoot up short ends
- Check that camera log book is being kept up to date
- Complete day's work
- Discuss first setup for the next day
- Ensure camera, electrical and grip crews get all copies of equipment rental or purchase invoices and approve before accountants pay vendors
- Take care of any future or ongoing production issues
- Answer any questions about future problems
- Visit production manager and producer at end of day
- Check for return of all unused equipment

G. Quality Control
- Call in for lab report
- View previous day's work in projected dailies with director, producer, editor, camera crew
- Discuss and approve dailies
- Consult with makeup, wardrobe, production designer and assistant director about dailies
- View, discuss, correct or approve second-unit or effects dailies
- Order reprints if necessary

H. Training
- Teach beginning actors movie technique (hitting marks, size of frame, lenses, etc.)

- Train camera crew for next job up the ladder

I. Contingency
- If director is disabled, finish day's shooting for him or her

III. PostProduction

A. Additional Photography
- Discuss and be aware of delivery dates for all postproduction
- Photograph or approve any additional scenes, inserts, special effects or second-unit footage

B. Timing (Color and Density)
- Time and approve trailer for theaters and TV
- Approve all optical and digital effects composites
- Time the picture
- Retime until correct

C. Quality Control
- Approve final answer print
- Show to director for ok
- Approve interpositive (IP)
- Approve internegatives (IN)
- Approve release prints
- Approve show prints from original negative
- Approve all blowups or reductions

D. Telecine/Color Correction
- Supervise and approve film or digital original transfer to electronic or film media (Hi-Def, NTSC, PAL, Secam masters, digital intermediates, archival masters, etc.)
- Supervise and approve all transfers to and from digital intermediates (DI)
- Supervise and approve all letterbox, pan and scan, or reformatting of film
- Supervise and approve tape-to-tape color correction and VHS, DVD, digital projection media, etc.
- Show electronic transfers to director for ok

E. Publicity
- Do any publicity (newspaper, magazine, Internet, radio, TV, DVD commentary, etc.)

F. Restoration/Archival
- Be available for any future reissue, archival reprint or electronic transfer of film

Summary of Formats

compiled by Tak Miyagishima
ASC Associate Member

APERTURE SPECIFICATIONS

35mm Camera - Spherical Lens

Academy Camera Aperture	.866" X .630"	22mm X 16mm

35mm Theatrical Release - Spherical

1.37:1	.825" X .602"	20.96mm X 15.29mm
1.66:1	.825" X .497"	20.96mm X 12.62mm
1.85:1	.825" X .446"	20.96mm X 11.33mm

35mm Television Aperture and Safe Areas

Camera Aperture	.866" X .630"	22mm X 16mm
TV Station Projector Aperture	.816" X .612"	20.73mm X 15.54mm
TV Transmitted Area	.792" X .594"	20.12mm X 15.09mm
TV Safe Action Area	.713" X .535"	18.11mm X 13.59mm
	Corner Radii = .143" / 3.63mm	
TV Safe Title Area	.630" X .475"	16mm X 12.06mm
	Corner Radii = .125" / 3.17mm	

35mm Full Aperture - Spherical Lens (For Partial Frame Extraction) Prints (Super 35)

Camera Aperture (Film Center)	.980" X .735"	24.89mm X 18.67mm
Finder Markings		
35mm Anamorphic 2.4:1 AR	.945" X .394"	24mm X 10mm
70mm 2.2:1 AR	.945" X .430"	24mm X 10.92mm
35mm FLAT 1.85:1 AR	.945" X .511"	24mm x 12.97mm

35mm Panavision 2-Perf

Camera Aperture (Film Center)	.980" X .365"	24.89mm x 9.27mm
Ground Glass 2.4:1 AR	.825" X .345"	20.96mm x 8.76mm

35mm Panavision 3-Perf

Camera Aperture (Film Center)	.980" X .546"	24.89mm x 13.87mm
1.78:1	.910" X .511"	23.10mm x 12.98mm

35mm Panavision 4-Perf

1.85:1 AR Spherical (FLAT) PROJ AP	.825" X .446"	20.96mm X 11.33mm
2.4:1 AR Anamorphic Squeeze PROJ AP	.825" X .690"	20.96mm X 17.53mm
5 perf 70mm 2.2:1 AR PROJ AP	1.912" X .870"	48.56mm X 22.10mm

Panavision 35 and Anamorphic Squeezed Negative

Camera Aperture	.866" X .732"	22mm X 18.59mm
35mm Squeezed Print		
Finder Marking (2.2:1 70mm) & Proj AP	.825" X .690"	20.96mm X 17.53mm
16mm Squeezed Print	.342" X .286"	8.69mm X 7.26mm
	Max Proj. AP	
16mm Un-Squeezed Print (1.85:1)	.380" X .205"	9.65mm X 5.20mm
	Proj. AP matte	
70mm Unsqueezed Print Proj. AP	1.912" X .870"	48.56mm X 22.10mm

APERTURE SPECIFICATIONS

16mm Film Apertures
1.33:1 (4:3) Television Safe Area

Camera Aperture	.404" X .295"	10.26mm X 7.49mm
TV Station Proj AP	.380" X .286"	9.65mm X 7.26mm
TV Transmitted Area	.368" X .276"	9.35mm X 7.01mm
TV Safe Action Area	.331" X .248"	8.41mm X 6.30mm
	Corner Radii R = .066"/1.68mm	
Safe Title Area	.293" X .221"	7.44mm X 5.61mm

16mm Finder Markings for Enlarging to 35mm

Camera Aperture	.404" X .295"	10.26mm X 7.49mm
Projector Aperture (1.37:1)	.380" X .286"	9.65mm X 7.26mm
Projector Aperture (1.85:1)	.380" X .206"	9.65mm X 5.23mm
(Enlarging ratio 1:2.105)		

Super 16mm (16mm Type W) for Enlarging to 35mm

Camera Aperture	.486" X .292"	12.35mm X 7.42mm
Projector Aperture (1.66)	.464" X .279"	11.80mm X 7.10mm
Projector Aperture (1.85)	.464" X .251"	11.80mm X 6.38mm

65mm 5-Perf
TODD-AO/PANAVISION 65mm Spherical Imaged Negative

Camera Aperture	2.072" X .906"	52.63mm X 23.01mm
70mm Projection Aperture 2.2:1	1.912" X .870"	48.56mm X 22.10mm
35mm 'Scope Extraction	1.912" X .800"	48.56mm X 20.31mm
35mm Projector Aperture	.825" X .690"	20.96mm X 17.53mm
		(with 2:1 squeeze)

65mm 8-Perf

Camera Aperture 1.35:1AR	2.072" X .1.485"	52.63mm X 37.72mm

65mm - 15-Perf IMAX/OMNIMAX

Camera Aperture	2.772" X 2.072"	70.41mm X 52.63mm
Projector Aperture (computed from cut-off)	1.172" X 2.04"	29.77mm X 51.81mm
16mm Un-Squeezed Print (1.85:1)	.380" X .206"	9.65mm X 5.20mm
70mm Unsqueezed Print Proj. AP	1.912" X .870"	48.56mm X 22.10mm

35mm - VISTAVISION 8-Perf Horizontal Pull Across

Camera Aperture	1.485" X .981"	37.72mm X 24.92mm
35mm VistaVision		

Super 8mm

Camera Aperture (1.33:1)	0.224" x 0.166"	5.69mm X 4.22mm
Projection Aperture (1.33:1)	0.209" x 0.158"	5.31mm X 4.01mm

1.37
(1.33 TV)

1.85

2.40

Most common screen ratios.

A Jumpstart Guide for the Student Cinematographer

by Stephen H. Burum, ASC

For many years I have felt that there should be a short, uncomplicated explanation of cinematography's basic underlying principles. Students should be able to start shooting right away, instead of reading or listening to arcane and complex treatises on photography.

The basics of cinematography are simple to grasp. They have been made this way by the tireless efforts of many scientists and working professionals who have created systems that ensure high-quality, repeatable results. The mathematical relationships in these systems are the keys to understanding how things work.

This brief article will quickly start you on the road to making pictures. Then when you have questions, the explanations and charts in our American Cinematographer Manual will provide the answers you seek.

It is the "art" of cinematography that is not so simple. This requires judgment, taste and experience.

Light

Let's start at the beginning with the element that is essential to our art: light. Whether it's natural (the sun) or artificial (electric lights), light is described by its color and intensity.

Color is identified in photographic terms either by color temperature in degrees Kelvin or by Mireds. The higher the color temperature, the bluer the light: the lower the color temperature, the redder the light. For cinematographers, the two most useful values to remember are Photographic Daylight Balance (5500°K) and Photographic Tungsten Balance (3200°K).

You'll also need to know the intensity of the light to determine your correct exposure. When you measure light bouncing off a subject, it is called reflected light, and its intensity is measured in footlamberts or candles per square meter. Light falling onto the subject is called incident light, and its intensity is measured in foot-candles or Lux.

Lenses

Light is focused through a lens to form an image on film. Lenses have a first and last name (e.g., 75mm f/1.4). The first name is its focal length in millimeters (mm). The second name is the maximum size its aperture will open to let in light (f/1.4).

The focal length is the distance from the optical center of the lens to the film plane where an image is formed when focused at infinity.

The aperture is the hole that controls the amount of light passing through the lens. There are a prescribed series of aperture sizes, each with a different numeric value. When these sets of values are derived by using a mathematical ratio between the size of the hole and the focal length of the lens, they are called f-stops. When these values are calibrated by measuring the light transmitted through the lens, they are called T-stops. Each of these values has the same function of describing the change in the amount of light from one stop to another. Each stop change either doubles or halves the light. Both f- and T-stops are the same for our purpose. These numbers have been standardized and their full value has been rounded off to the following numbers we see engraved on our lens. Starting at the biggest hole and proceeding to the smallest hole, they are: 1.4, 2, 2.8, 4, 5.6, 8, 11, 16 and 22.

Every lens has a set of characteristics. Its angle of view is how much the lens sees of both its horizontal and vertical angles. Its depth of field is the distance between points nearest to and farthest from the camera that look sharp. To get more depth of field: 1. use a smaller format, 2. smaller aperture, 3. shorter focal length, 4. move the point of focus farther from camera. For less depth of field: 1. use a larger format, 2. bigger aperture, 3. longer focal length, 4. move the point of focus closer to camera. The lens's perspective drawing shows the three-dimensional relationship of the depth between objects in the frame. These characteristics work together and can be altered for dramatic effect by using lenses with different focal lengths.

The normal lens is one that creates a perspective similar to human vision so that the depth between objects appears as a human would see it. Each film size or format has a corresponding normal lens, which is said to have a focal length equal to the diagonal of the format. In full-aperture 35mm motion-picture photography, the normal lens's focal length is about 32mm, and in the 16mm format it's about 13mm.

Lenses with a focal length of less than normal are called either short or wide-angle lenses. Lenses with a greater-than-normal focal length are called long or telephoto lenses. When placed side by side, the wide-angle lens sees more area at the same distance than a normal lens. The long lens sees less area at this distance than either the wide-angle or normal lenses.

By using different focal lengths, the size relationship between objects in the frame can be altered. If you keep the distance between two objects the same, and the foreground object the same size with each different lens, you will notice that using a wide-angle lens makes the background object appear smaller than it does with a normal lens. If you use a telephoto lens, you will see that the foreground and background objects appear to be very close to the same size. The impression that different lenses have different perspective drawings is a function of its angle of view.

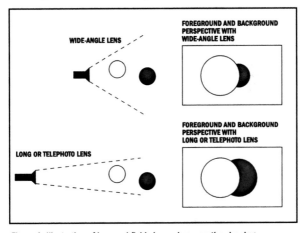

Figure 1. Illustration of lens and field size and perspective drawing.

Black-and-White Film

Pictures are formed by light being focused onto a clear, flexible film coated with silver halide. This material is light-sensitive. When struck by light a chemical change occurs, forming a latent image. After the film is developed, the silver is left on the film base in the same proportion as the amount of light striking it. The brighter the subject, the more silver is left; the darker the subject, the less silver is left. The exposed silver forms a negative or reverse image. To see the correct tonal representation of the scene, a positive print must be made from the negative.

Color Film

Color pictures are made by using three layers of black-and-white emulsion. Each layer is made sensitive to only one of the three primary colors of light: Red, Green and Blue. Each of these layers contains a different color dye that couples with the exposed silver to reproduce the colors we see.

Electronic Photography

Instead of changing chemicals into silver and dye, light is focused onto a light-sensitive tube or chip that changes light into electricity. These voltages are translated through circuitry to produce pictures. (See ASC Video Manual.)

Color Theory

Both color and panchromatic black-and-white film are sensitive to the three primary colors of light: Red, Green and Blue. There are also three complementary or opposite colors: Cyan, Magenta and Yellow. Please note their relationship in the chart below:

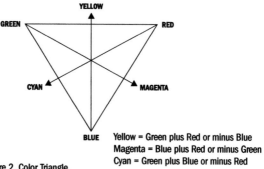

Yellow = Green plus Red or minus Blue
Magenta = Blue plus Red or minus Green
Cyan = Green plus Blue or minus Red

Figure 2. Color Triangle.

Filters

If you place a colored filter over your camera lens it will block out the light of its complement. For example, a yellow filter will only transmit red and green light and will block the blue light. Blocking or subtracting colors is the keystone of black-and-white contrast and tonal control. It is also the basis of color correction in color photography. Filters require an exposure increase because of light loss. Special colorless (neutral) filters used to reduce exposure are called Neutral Density or ND filters. The amount of increase is indicated by the filter factor. (See Kodak Publications H-1, B-3, H-188 and KW-13.)

Filter Factors

Equivalent F-Stop Corrections for Filter Factors

Filter Factor	Increase In Stops	Filter Factor	Increase In Stops
1.25	+ $\frac{1}{3}$	8	+ 3
1.5	+ $\frac{2}{3}$	10	+ 3 $\frac{1}{3}$
2	+ 1	12	+ 3 $\frac{2}{3}$
2.5	+ 1 $\frac{1}{3}$	16	+ 4
3	+ 1 $\frac{2}{3}$	40	+ 5 $\frac{1}{3}$
4	+ 2	100	+ 6 $\frac{2}{3}$
5	+ 2 $\frac{1}{3}$	1000	+ 10
6	+ 2 $\frac{2}{3}$	10,000	+ 13 $\frac{1}{3}$

Figure 3. Filter Factors are in $\frac{1}{3}$ stops.

Neutral Density Filters

Kodak Wratten Neutral Density Filter No. 96

Neutral Density	Percent Transmittance	Filter Factor	Increase in Exposure (Stops)
0.1	80	1.25	+ $\frac{1}{3}$
0.2	63	1.5	+ $\frac{2}{3}$
0.3	50	2	+1
0.4	40	2.5	+1 $\frac{1}{3}$
0.5	32	3	+1 $\frac{2}{3}$
0.6	25	4	+2
0.7	20	5	+2 $\frac{1}{3}$
0.8	16	6	+2 $\frac{2}{3}$
0.9	13	8	+3
1.0	10	10	+3 $\frac{1}{3}$
2.0	1	100	+6 $\frac{2}{3}$
3.0	0.1	1,000	+10
4.0	0.01	10,000	+13 $\frac{1}{3}$

Figure 4. Neutral density filters are graded in $\frac{1}{3}$ stops.

Film Speed

Every film stock requires a specific amount of light to make its best picture. Film manufacturers have a rating system called an Exposure Index, or EI, that tells you what this quantity of light will be. The higher the number, the less light is required. This number is also referred to as ASA, ISO or, in Europe, DIN. It can be found on the film label.

Each one of these numbers changes the exposure ⅓ of a stop. (See Kodak publication H-740.)

EI/ASA				
6	**25**	**100**	**400**	**1600**
8	32	125	500	2000
10	40	160	640	2500
12	**50**	**200**	**800**	**3200**
16	64	250	1000	4000
20	80	320	1250	5000

Figure 5. EI/ASA. Film speed ratings are in ⅓ stops.

Charts relating to the number of footcandles needed for a particular exposure index (EI, ASA, ISO) at a certain f-stop are arranged in ⅓-stop increments. (See charts on pages 100–102.)

F/T-Stops

F-stop and T-stop numbers represent a relationship of how much light you are letting into or cutting out of the lens. Each stop either doubles or halves the light. If you open up one stop [bigger hole, smaller number], you let in twice as much light. If you close down one stop [smaller hole, bigger number], you decrease the light falling on the film by one half. When you open up or close down by more than one stop, you multiply the doubling and halving effect.

The relationships of all these variables can be correlated so you can move between values to fine-tune your exposure system. They all use the common unit of ⅓ stop of exposure.

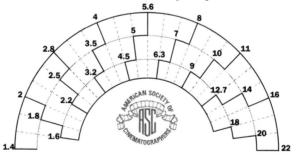

Figure 6. F/T-Stops in ⅓ stops. Shows at a glance lens settings to increase or decrease aperture ⅓,⅔ or 1 stop when using filters or shooting above or below normal speed. Each division in same arc band represents one full stop each radiating step represents one third stop.

F/T-Stop Relations		
	Open (increase)	**Closed (decrease)**
1 Stop	2 x 1 = 2	$\frac{1}{2}$ x 1 = $\frac{1}{2}$
2 Stops	2 x 2 = 4	$\frac{1}{2}$ x $\frac{1}{2}$ = $\frac{1}{4}$
3 Stops	2 x 2 x 2 = 8	$\frac{1}{2}$ x $\frac{1}{2}$ x $\frac{1}{2}$ = $\frac{1}{8}$
4 Stops	2 x 2 x 2 x 2 = 16	$\frac{1}{2}$ x $\frac{1}{2}$ x $\frac{1}{2}$ x $\frac{1}{2}$ = $\frac{1}{16}$

Figure 7. F/T-Stop Relations

Exposure Time

Exposure time has two components: the angle of the shutter opening expressed in degrees, and the number of frames that pass by the camera aperture in frames per second. Sound movie cameras run at 24 frames per second, at a standard shutter opening from about 170 degrees to 200 degrees. To get the exposure time in fractions of a second, simply double the frame rate. In the case of 24 fps it would be $\frac{1}{48}$ of a second, but it is always rounded off to $\frac{1}{50}$ of a second. If you alter the shutter opening or the frame rate, your exposure time will change. (See formula on page 34.)

Film Facts

Size of film	Frames per foot	Feet per minute at 24 fps
Super 8mm	72	20
16mm	40	36
35mm	16	90
65/70mm	12.8	112 feet + 6.4 frames
VistaVision (sideways35mm double frame)	8	180

The Camera

Most professional movie cameras have the following components: 1. a focusable lens with variable f-stops; 2. a light tight box; 3. a shutter to black out the film while it moves to the next frame; 4. an intermittent movement to hold motionless and register the film for a split-second exposure; 5. a film transport to move the film through the camera (motor); 6. a magazine to hold the film; 7. a viewing system that is either reflex (looking through the lens), non-reflex (looking through an external finder), or electronic (a little TV screen); 8. a follow focus control; 9. a matte box to shade lens and hold filters; 10. a footage and frame counter; 11. a tachometer to show frame rate; 12. shutter angle indicator.

The camera can be mounted on several types of moveable heads that can pan and tilt the camera; 1. friction head; 2. gear head; 3. fluid head; 4. remote head; 5. third axis head; 6. computer-controlled recording and playback head (for motion control), 7. computer stabilized head.

The camera and head are then mounted on: 1.tripod; 2. dolly (wheeled platform to move camera); 3.crane (teeter-totter device to move the camera up and down); 4. self-leveling gimbal base; 5. special mounts lashed to cars, boats and planes; 6. a self-stabilizing mount, like a Steadicam. Finally, you can just hold the camera by itself (handheld).

Getting Started

Now let's put together what we need to know to start shooting. Is your film color balanced for daylight or tungsten? Most professional color movie film is balanced for tungsten. If you are shooting under a daylight source (sunlight, arcs, HMI, daylight fluorescent tubes or color-corrected tungsten light), you will need to put a filter on the film to get the proper color balance. To convert tungsten-balanced color film (3200°K) to daylight balance (5500°K), use the Wratten number 85 filter. If your light source is tungsten-balanced, then just shoot away. For black-and-white film, choose the EI that represents your light balance. Because black-and-white film is more sensitive to blue light, you will notice the daylight EI is higher than the tungsten. No color temperature correction is necessary, but you may want to use a contrast-control filter outside. As noted earlier, each film stock has a film sensitivity (speed) rating called the exposure index (EI, ASA, ISO or DIN). You will find this information on the film can along with the color balance.

Set your light meter to the correct EI rating that is on the film-can label. There are two EIs, one for daylight and one for tungsten. Your meter also has a series of exposure times marked as shutter speeds. If you are shooting at sound speed, your exposure will be ⅟₅₀ of a second. Next, if you have a reflective meter, point it at the scene from the camera. If you have an incident meter, stand at your subject and point it at the camera. If you have no meter and you are outside on a bright sunny day, use the still photography f/16 rule: *"If your subject is in full front light, set your shutter speed (exposure time) at the EI of the film. The f-stop will be f/16."* You know that for sound movies the shutter speed (exposure time) is a constant ⅟₅₀. If your EI is 50, your lens can be set at f/16, as seen in the chart below. If your EI is different, simply use the tables in the manual to come up with the correct exposure.

Daylight Exposure for 50 EI/ASA at ⅟₅₀ of a second	
Bright or hazy sun on light sand or snow	f/22
Bright or hazy sun (distinct shadows)	f/16
Weak hazy sun (soft shadows)	f/11
Cloudy bright (no shadows)	f/8
Heavy overcast or open shade	f/5.6
Backlight close-up	f/5.6
Subject brighter than normal: close down ½ to 1 stop Subject darker than normal: open up ½ to 1 stop	

Figure 8. Daylight Exposure

Lighting Basics

Making two-dimensional works of art (such as paintings, still photographs and motion pictures) appear three-dimensional is done by using classic lighting techniques developed by artists over hundreds of years.

First, cast a shadow. This gives your subject form and texture. The edge of the shadow is defined by the light source you use. A pinpoint source gives a sharp edge similar to the sun. A large area source makes a soft, diffused edge that almost melts away as on an overcast day. There are many gradations in between. The light source is called the keylight.

To create depth, you must separate one object from another (people from walls, etc.). This can only be done by contrasting light against dark or dark against light. This is true whether you work in black-and-white or color. The lights used to do this are called backlights, kickers, rims, liners and glow lights.

In order to create a mood, you must control the detail in the shadows you've cast by adding or subtracting light from these shadows. This is called fill light.

Exposure is always determined by reading the value of the keylight. The other lights are judged by eye against the value of the keylight.

The volume of lights and darks you put in the frame will help you set the time and mood of the story (e.g., lots of dark tones for night, lots of light tones for day). The time of day and season of the year are indicated by the angle of the sun. At sunrise and sunset we know that the light is low on the horizon, and at noon it is high overhead. We also know that the noon sun is lower in the winter and higher in the summer.

Finally, if you want your picture to look rich, it must have a full range of values; each frame needs a black reference, a white reference and a key or middle-gray reference. These may be only small portions of the screen, but if they are missing your scene will look flat and uninteresting. This is especially true for black-and-white. (See *Reflections: Twenty-One Cinematographers at Work,* by Benjamin Bergery.)

Testing

Testing for the cinematographer is like practice for a dancer or rehearsal for an actor: the more you do it, the better you get. There is no substitute for the knowledge and understanding you get from testing. All of the voluminous books and charts are only a starting point for learning the art and craft of cinematography. So let's get to work.

LABORATORY FLOW CHART

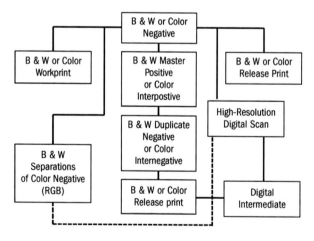

Formulas

By R. Evans Wetmore. P. E. ASC Associate Member

1 Lens Formulas

The formulas given in this section are sufficiently accurate to solve most practical problems encountered in cinematography. Many of the equations, however, are approximations or simplifications of very complex optical relationships. Therefore, shooting tests should always be considered when using these formulas, especially in critical situations.

1.1 Hyperfocal Distance

The hyperfocal distance (H) is the focus distance setting of a lens where all objects from half the focus distance setting through infinity are in acceptable focus. Acceptable focus is characterized by a parameter called the circle of confusion (C_c). The lens aperture setting and the circle of confusion affect the hyperfocal distance. The formula for hyperfocal distance is:

$$H = \frac{F^2}{fC_c} \tag{1}$$

where F = focal length of lens
f = f-stop of lens
C_c = circle of confusion

All values in this and the following equations must be in the same units, e.g., millimeters, inches, etc. For instance, when using a circle of confusion value measured in inches, the lens focal length must be in inches, and the resulting answer will be in inches. (Note: f-stop has no dimensions and so is not affected by the type of units used.)

As mentioned above, the circle of confusion characterizes the degree of acceptable focus. The smaller the circle of confusion is the higher the resulting image sharpness. For practical purposes the following values have been used in computing depth of field and hyperfocal distances in this manual:

35mm photography = 0.001 inch ($\frac{1}{1000}$ inch) or 0.025mm

16mm photography = 0.0005 inch ($\frac{5}{10,000}$ inch) or 0.013mm

TAK'S TIPS		
Multiplication Constants for Calculating Hyperfocal Distance for Circle of Confusions in Feet		
CC (in Inches)	**Decimal of CC**	**Constant**
1/500	0.002	0.06458
1/707	0.0014	0.09226
1/1000	0.001	0.12917
1/1414	0.0007	0.18452
1/1666	0.0006	0.21528
1/2500	0.0005	0.32292
Example: For CC = .0005 $F = 35mm\ f/4$ $H = \dfrac{.32292 \times 35^2}{4} = 98.89'$		

1.2 Depth of Field

For a discussion on the concept of depth of field, please see the introduction to the Depth of Field Tables. It should be understood that the detemination of depth of field involves a subjective judgement that requires taking into account the conditions under which the final projected image will be viewed.

The following two formulas are for calculating the depth of field. To use these equations one must first calculate the hyperfocal distance from Equation 1.

$$D_n = \frac{HS}{H + (S - F)} \tag{2}$$

$$D_f = \frac{HS}{H - (S - F)} \tag{3}$$

where D_n = Camera to Near Limit
D_f = Camera to Far Limit
H = Hyperfocal Distance

S = Distance from Camera to Subject
F = Focal Length of Lens

The total depth of field is equal to D_f - D_n.

The following shows how the above equations can be used to make hyperfocal and depth of field calculations:

Example: A 35 mm camera lens of 50 mm focal length is focused at 20 feet and is set to f/2.8. Over what range of distances will objects be in acceptable focus?

First convert all the units to the same system. In this example inches will be used. Therefore, the 50 mm focal length will be converted to 2 inches. (This is an approximation as 50 mm is exactly 1.969 inches, but 2 inches is close enough for normal work.) Also the 20 feet converts to 240 inches (20 $\times$ 12). The circle of confusion is 0.001 inches for 35 mm photography.

Using Equation 1 and filling in the converted values yields:

$$H = \frac{2^2}{2.8 \times 0.001} = \frac{4}{0.0028} = 1429 \text{ inches} = 119 \text{ feet}$$

Using the hyperfocal distance just calculated and equations 2 and 3, we can now calculate the near and far distances that will be in acceptable focus.

$$D_n = \frac{1429 \times 240}{1429 + (240 - 2)} = 205.7 \text{ inches} = 17.1 \text{ feet}$$

$$D_f = \frac{1429 \times 240}{1429 - (240 - 2)} = 288 \text{ inches} = 24.0 \text{ feet}$$

Therefore, when a 50 mm lens at f/2.8 is focused at 20 feet, everything from 17.1 feet to 24.0 feet will be in acceptable focus. The total depth of field for this example is:

$$D_{total} = D_f - D_n = 24.0 - 17.1 = 6.9 \text{ feet}$$

If a more approximate answer is all that is needed, equations 2 and 3 may be simplified to:

$$D_n = \frac{HS}{H + S} \tag{4}$$

$$D_f = \frac{HS}{H - S} \tag{5}$$

Using these equations, D_n and D_f are

$$D_n = \frac{119 \times 20}{119 + 20} \approx 17 \text{ feet}$$

$$D_f = \frac{119 \times 20}{119 - 20} \approx 24 \text{ feet}$$

Therefore, $D_{total} = 24 - 17 = 7$ feet

TAK'S TIPS
SIMPLIFIED DEPTH OF FIELD
$\dfrac{1}{D_n} = \dfrac{1}{S} + \dfrac{1}{H}$
$\dfrac{1}{D_f} = \dfrac{1}{S} - \dfrac{1}{H}$
D_n = Camera to Near Limit D_f = Camera to Far Limit H = Hyperfocal Distance S = Distance from Camera to Subject

Courtesy of Panavision's Tak Miyagishima.

1.2.1 Finding Lens Settings When Dn and Df are Known

When the near and far focus requirements are known, equations 4, 5 and 1 can be rearranged as follows:

$$L_s = \frac{2D_n D_f}{D_n + D_f} \tag{6}$$

$$H = \frac{2D_n D_f}{D_f - D_n} \qquad (7)$$

$$f = \frac{F^2}{HC_c} \qquad (8)$$

where D_n = Camera to Near Limit
D_f = Camera to Far Limit
H = Hyperfocal Distance
L_s = Lens Focus Distance Setting
F = Focal Length of Lens
f = f-stop Setting of Lens
C_c = circle of confusion

Example: A scene is being photographed on 35mm using a 75 mm lens. Everything in the scene from 15 to 27 feet must be in acceptable focus. How must the lens f-stop and focus be set?

First convert all distances and focal lengths to inches. Focal length is 2.953 inches (75 ÷ 25.40). D_n is 180 inches (15 × 12), and D_f is 324 inches (27 × 12).

$$L_s = \text{focus distance setting} = \frac{2 \times 180 \times 324}{180 + 324} = 231 \text{ inches} = 19.3 \text{ feet}$$

$$H = \text{hyperfocal distance} = \frac{2 \times 180 \times 324}{324 - 180} = 810 \text{ inches} = 67.5 \text{ feet}$$

$$\text{f-stop} = \frac{2.953^2}{0.001 \times 810} = \text{f/10.77} \approx 19.3 \text{ feet}$$

Therefore, focus the lens to 19.3 feet, and set the f-stop to f/11.

1.3 Depth of Focus

Depth of Focus should not be confused with Depth of Field as they are very different and do *not* refer to the same thing.

Depth of Focus is the range of distance between the lens and the film plane where acceptable focus is maintained. This range is quite small and is measured usually in very small units such as thousands of an inch.

For an image to be in sharp focus, the distance from the lens to the film must be held to very tight tolerances, hence the design of motion-picture cameras which holds the film very securely during exposure. Any buckling of the film or anything that shifts the film's postition in the aperture can cause a deterioration of focus.

The following equation provides a good approximation of the depth of focus of a lens:

$$\text{Depth of Focus} \approx \frac{Ff}{1000}$$

(9)

where $F =$ focal length of lens (in mm)
$f = $ f-stop of lens

Example: A 50 mm f/2.8 lens has the following depth of focus:

$$\frac{50 \times 2.8}{1000} = 0.14 \text{ mm} = 0.0055 \text{ inch}$$

As this is the total depth of focus, the film must stay within plus or minus half that value which is about ±0.00275 inch or ±0.07 mm. This dimension is equal to the approximate value of a single strand of human hair. This is a very small value indeed which further amplifies the statement above about the need for precision in the gate and aperture area of the camera.

1.4 Lens Viewing Angles

The angle, either horizonal or vertical, that a lens images onto the film frame may be calculated using the following equation:

$$\Theta = 2 \, atan \left(\frac{ARs}{2F} \right)$$

where $F =$ focal length of lens   **(10)**
$A =$ camera aperture height or width
$Rs =$ squeeze ratio (use 1.0 for spherical lenses and Scope vertical and use 2.0 for Scope horizontal) *scope is anamorphic*
$\Theta =$ viewing angle

The inverse tangent (written as atan, arctan, or tan-1) can be found with many pocket calculators. Alternately Table 1 relates atan to Θ

Example: What are horizontal and vertical viewing angles for a 75mm Scope lens?

Inverse Tangent Function							
Angle	**atan**	**Angle**	**atan**	**Angle**	**atan**	**Angle**	**atan**
1°	.018	12°	.213	23°	.424	34°	.675
2°	.035	13°	.231	24°	.445	35°	.700
3°	.052	14°	.249	25°	.466	36°	.727
4°	.070	15°	.268	26°	.488	37°	.754
5°	.088	16°	.287	27°	.510	38°	.781
6°	.105	17°	.306	28°	.532	39°	.810
7°	.123	18°	.325	29°	.554	40°	.839
8°	.141	19°	.344	30°	.577	41°	.869
9°	.158	20°	.364	31°	.601	42°	.900
10°	.176	21°	.384	32°	.625	43°	.933
11°	.194	22°	.404	33°	.649	44°	.966
						45°	1.000

Table 1: *atan* Table

A typical Scope camera aperture is 0.868" wide by 0.735" high. Converting 75 mm to inches yields 2.953 inches ($75 \div 25.4 = 2.953$)

$$\text{Horizontal Angle} = 2 \, atan \; \frac{0.868 \times 2.0}{2 \times 2.953} = 32.8°$$

$$\text{Vertical Angle} = 2 \, atan \; \frac{0.735 \times 1.0}{2 \times 2.953} = 14.2°$$

1.5 Lens, Subject, Distance, and Image Size Relationships

Using the following simple drawing, the relationships between camera distance, object size, image size, and lens focal length for spherical lenses may easily be calculated in the following equation:

$$\frac{O}{A} = \frac{D}{F} \tag{11}$$

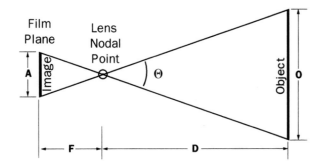

where   F = focal length of lens
D = distance to object being photographed
O = size of object being photographed
A = aperture size
Θ = viewing angle

Equation 11 may be rewritten in any of the following ways depending on the problem being solved:

$$D = \frac{OF}{A} \tag{12}$$

$$O = \frac{AD}{F} \tag{13}$$

$$F = \frac{AD}{O} \tag{14}$$

$$A = \frac{OF}{D} \tag{15}$$

2 Shooting Practices

2.1 Running Times, Feet, and Frames

Table 2 shows the linear sound speed (24fps) of common theatrical film gages and the number of frames per foot.

Film Gage (in mm)	Linear Speed (ft/min)	Frames per Foot
16	36	40
35	90	16
65/70	112.5	12.8

Table 2: Speed and Frame Information for Common Film Gages

2.1.1 Footage versus Time Relationship

$$T_F = St$$

where T_F = total footage
S = speed of film (in ft/min)
t = time (in minutes)

Example: How many feet of 35 mm film run through a sound camera in 4 and a half minutes?

$$T_F = 90 \times 4.5 = 405 \text{ feet}$$

2.1.2 Footage in Feet and Frames

$$F_T = \frac{t\,F_s}{F_F}$$

where F_T = total footage
F_s = frames per second
t = time (in seconds)
F_F = frames per foot

Example: How much film goes through a 16 mm sound camera in 8 seconds?

$$F_T = \frac{8 \times 24}{40} = 4.8 \text{ feet}$$

To convert the decimal to frames, multiply the decimal part by number of frames per foot:

$$.8 \times 40 = 32$$

Therefore, the answer is 4 feet 32 frames.

2.2 Computing Exposure Times

The following equations relates frame rate, shutter angle, and exposure time:

$$T_e = \frac{1}{\frac{S\,360}{\alpha}} \qquad \text{and} \quad \alpha = 360 S T_e$$

where α = shutter angle (in degrees)
       S = frames per second
       T_e = exposure time (in seconds)

Example: What is the exposure time when shooting at 24 frames per second with a 180° shutter?

$$T_e = \frac{1}{\frac{24 \times 360}{180}}$$

$$\frac{1}{\frac{8640}{180}} = \frac{1}{48} \text{ second}$$

2.3 Frame Rates for Miniatures

To make the action in miniatures look convincing, it is often necessary to shoot at frame rates faster than 24 fps. The exact frame rate for a given miniature shot must be determined by shooting test footage. Even skilled minature cinematographers will shoot tests to confirm proper effect on film.

Shooting frame rate depends on, among other things, subject matter, direction of movement in relation to the camera position, and minature scale. Generally, however, the smaller the minature, the faster the required frame rate. Also as magnification decreases, the necessary frame rate drops.

The following may be used as a guide and a starting point:

$$R_f = 24 \sqrt{\frac{1}{S}}$$

where R_f = frame rate
           S = scale of miniature

Example: What frame rate should be used to shoot a 1:4 (quarter scale) miniature?

$$R_f = 24 \sqrt{\frac{1}{0.25}} = 24 \sqrt{4} = 24 \times 2 = 48 \text{ fps}$$

OPTICAL LENS EXTENDER EXPOSURE FACTORS

1.4X = Factor of 2 − 1 Stop increase
1.6X = Factor of 2.5 − 1 ⅓ Stop Increase
2X = Factor of 4 − 2 Stop Increase
Magnification squared = Factor
Example: 1.4 x 1.4 = 1.96 closest factor 2

Non-Optical Extension Tube or Bellows Exposure Factors

Distance of lens from film plane squared, divided by the focal length squared = factor.

Example:
50mm lens + 50mm extension = factor of 4
2 stop increase

$$\frac{(50 + 50)^2}{50^2} = \frac{10,000}{2500} = 4$$

Depth of Field
Tables Introduction

by R. Evans Wetmore P.E.
ASC Associate Member

These comprehensive "All Formats Depth of Field Tables" will provide you with depth of field information for selected 16, 35, and 65mm lenses. You will also find tables for Super 8mm and additional 16mm tables beginning on page 76.

These tables are computed mathematically, and should be used as a guide only.

Technically speaking, an object is only in focus at one precise point in space. Depth of field determines the range in front of and behind a designated focusing distance, where an object still appears to be acceptably in focus. A low resolving film stock or lens may appear to have greater depth of field, because the "in focus" image is already so soft, it is more difficult to determine when it goes further out of focus. Conversely, a very sharp, high contrast lens may appear to have shallow depth of field, because the "in focus" image has such clarity, it is much easier to notice when it slips out of a range of acceptable focus.

That being said, these charts should be very helpful, unless you are trying to measure down to an accuracy of less than a couple of inches. If you are demanding that level of precision, then you must shoot a test of the lens in question, because no calculation can provide the empirical data a visual evaluation can.

These tables are calculated based on a circle of confusion of 0.001" ($\frac{1}{1000}$"). To calculate a depth of field based upon a more critical circle of confusion of half that size (0.0005" or $\frac{5}{10,000}$"), find your chosen f-stop at the distance desired, then read the depth of field data two columns to the left. The 0.0005" circle of confusion can be used for lenses of greater sharpness or contrast, or for a more traditional method of determining 16mm depth of field.

One more note: you will see some lenses at certain distances that indicate a depth of field of effectively nothing (e.g.: 10' 0" to 10' 0"). This means the depth of field is less than an inch, and we recommend that a test is shot to determine such a critical depth of field.

MEASUREMENT CONVERSION FACTORS

Use multiplying factor to convert from one system to the other.
Example: 6 feet x .3048 = 1.8288 meters.

English to Metric Factors		Metric to English Factors	
Yards to meters (m)	.914	Meters to yards (yd)	1.09
Feet to meters (m)	.3048	Meters to feet (ft)	3.28
Inches to millimeters (mm)	25.4	Centimeters to feet (ft)	.03281
Miles to kilometers (km)	1.61	Centimeters to inches (in)	.3937
Pounds to kilograms (kg)	.454	Millimeters to inches (in)	.0394
Ounces to grams (g)	28.4	Kilometers to miles (mi)	.621
Gallons to liters (l)	3.79	Kilograms to pounds (lb)	2.21
Quarts to liters (l)	.946	Grams to ounces (oz)	.0353
Fluid ounces to milliliters (ml)	29.6	Liters to gallons (gal)	.264
		Liters to quarts (qt)	1.06
		Milliliters to fluid ounces (fl oz)	.0338

1 inch = 25.4mm = 2.54cm = .0254m
1 foot = 304.8mm = 30.48cm = .3048m
1yard = .9144m

5.9mm — ALL FORMATS DEPTH OF FIELD TABLE — CIRCLE OF CONFUSION=0.0010 inches

FOCUS (feet)	f/1.4 NEAR/FAR	f/2 NEAR/FAR	f/2.8 NEAR/FAR	f/4 NEAR/FAR	f/5.6 NEAR/FAR	f/8 NEAR/FAR	f/11 NEAR/FAR	f/16 NEAR/FAR	f/22 NEAR/FAR
Hyper. Dist.	3'3"	2'3"	1'7"	1'1"	0'10"	0'7"	0'5"	0'3"	0'2"
2	1'3" / 5'3"	1'1" / INF	0'11" / INF	0'9" / INF	0'7" / INF	0'5" / INF	0'4" / INF	0'3" / INF	0'2" / INF
2½	1'5" / 11'0"	1'2" / INF	1'0" / INF	0'9" / INF	0'7" / INF	0'6" / INF	0'4" / INF	0'3" / INF	0'2" / INF
3	1'7" / INF	1'3" / INF	1'1" / INF	0'10" / INF	0'8" / INF	0'6" / INF	0'4" / INF	0'3" / INF	0'2" / INF
3½	1'8" / INF	1'4" / INF	1'1" / INF	0'10" / INF	0'8" / INF	0'6" / INF	0'4" / INF	0'3" / INF	0'2" / INF
4	1'9" / INF	1'5" / INF	1'2" / INF	0'11" / INF	0'8" / INF	0'6" / INF	0'4" / INF	0'3" / INF	0'2" / INF
4½	1'11" / INF	1'6" / INF	1'2" / INF	0'11" / INF	0'8" / INF	0'6" / INF	0'5" / INF	0'3" / INF	0'2" / INF
5	2'0" / INF	1'7" / INF	1'3" / INF	0'11" / INF	0'8" / INF	0'6" / INF	0'5" / INF	0'3" / INF	0'2" / INF
5½	2'0" / INF	1'7" / INF	1'3" / INF	0'11" / INF	0'8" / INF	0'6" / INF	0'5" / INF	0'3" / INF	0'2" / INF
6	2'1" / INF	1'8" / INF	1'3" / INF	0'11" / INF	0'9" / INF	0'6" / INF	0'5" / INF	0'3" / INF	0'2" / INF

6½	2'2" INF	1'8" INF	1'3" INF	1'0" INF	0'9" INF	0'6" INF	0'5" INF	0'3" INF	0'2" INF
7	2'2" INF	1'8" INF	1'4" INF	1'0" INF	0'9" INF	0'6" INF	0'5" INF	0'3" INF	0'2" INF
8	2'4" INF	1'9" INF	1'4" INF	1'0" INF	0'9" INF	0'6" INF	0'5" INF	0'3" INF	0'2" INF
9	2'4" INF	1'10" INF	1'4" INF	1'0" INF	0'9" INF	0'6" INF	0'5" INF	0'3" INF	0'2" INF
10	2'5" INF	1'10" INF	1'5" INF	1'0" INF	0'9" INF	0'6" INF	0'5" INF	0'3" INF	0'2" INF
12	2'6" INF	1'11" INF	1'5" INF	1'0" INF	0'9" INF	0'6" INF	0'5" INF	0'3" INF	0'2" INF
14	2'7" INF	1'11" INF	1'5" INF	1'1" INF	0'9" INF	0'6" INF	0'5" INF	0'3" INF	0'2" IN
16	2'8" INF	2'0" INF	1'6" INF	1'1" INF	0'9" INF	0'7" INF	0'5" INF	0'3" INF	0'2" INF
18	2'9" INF	2'0" INF	1'6" INF	1'1" INF	0'9" INF	0'7" INF	0'5" INF	0'3" INF	0'2" INF
20	2'9" INF	2'0" INF	1'6" INF	1'1" INF	0'9" INF	0'7" INF	0'5" INF	0'3" INF	0'2" INF
25	2'10" INF	2'1" INF	1'6" INF	1'1" INF	0'9" INF	0'7" INF	0'5"'' INF	0'3" INF	0'2" INF
50	3'0" INF	2'2" INF	1'7" INF	1'1" INF	0'9" INF	0'7" INF	0'5" INF	0'3" INF	0'2" INF

For circle of confusion = .0005 use depth data two columns left of chosen F-Stop.

10mm — ALL FORMATS DEPTH OF FIELD TABLE — CIRCLE OF CONFUSION=0.0010 inches

FOCUS (feet)	f/1.4 NEAR	f/1.4 FAR	f/2 NEAR	f/2 FAR	f/2.8 NEAR	f/2.8 FAR	f/4 NEAR	f/4 FAR	f/5.6 NEAR	f/5.6 FAR	f/8 NEAR	f/8 FAR	f/11 NEAR	f/11 FAR	f/16 NEAR	f/16 FAR	f/22 NEAR	f/22 FAR
Hyper. Dist.	9' 3"		6' 6"		4' 7"		3' 3"		2' 4"		1' 7"		1' 2"		0' 10"		0' 7"	
2	1' 8"	2' 7"	1' 6"	2' 11"	1' 5"	3' 6"	1' 3"	5' 1"	1' 1"	13' 7"	0' 11"	INF	0' 9"	INF	0' 7"	INF	0' 6"	INF
2 ½	2' 0"	3' 5"	1' 10"	4' 1"	1' 8"	5' 4"	1' 5"	10' 7"	1' 2"	INF	1' 0"	INF	0' 10"	INF	0' 7"	INF	0' 6"	INF
3	2' 3"	4' 5"	2' 1"	5' 7"	1' 10"	8' 5"	1' 7"	INF	1' 4"	INF	1' 1"	INF	0' 10"	INF	0' 8"	INF	0' 6"	INF
3 ½	2' 7"	5' 7"	2' 3"	7' 7"	2' 0"	14' 1"	1' 8"	INF	1' 5"	INF	1' 1"	INF	0' 11"	INF	0' 8"	INF	0' 6"	INF
4	2' 10"	7' 0"	2' 6"	10' 4"	2' 2"	28' 7"	1' 10"	INF	1' 6"	INF	1' 2"	INF	0' 11"	INF	0' 8"	INF	0' 6"	INF
4 ½	3' 0"	8' 9"	2' 8"	14' 7"	2' 3"	INF	1' 11"	INF	1' 6"	INF	1' 2"	INF	0' 11"	INF	0' 8"	INF	0' 6"	INF
5	3' 3"	10' 10"	2' 10"	21' 8"	2' 5"	INF	2' 0"	INF	1' 7"	INF	1' 3"	INF	1' 0"	INF	0' 8"	INF	0' 6"	INF
5 ½	3' 5"	13' 6"	3' 0"	35' 10"	2' 6"	INF	2' 1"	INF	1' 8"	INF	1' 3"	INF	1' 0"	INF	0' 8"	INF	0' 6"	INF
6	3' 8"	17' 0"	3' 1"	INF	2' 7"	INF	2' 1"	INF	1' 8"	INF	1' 3"	INF	1' 0"	INF	0' 9"	INF	0' 6"	INF

f-stop									
6½	3'10" 21'9"	3'3" INF	2'8" INF	2'2" INF	1'9" INF	1'4" INF	1'0" INF	0'9" INF	0'6" INF
7	4'0" 28'7"	3'4" INF	2'9" INF	2'3" INF	1'9" INF	1'4" INF	1'0" INF	0'9" INF	0'7" INF
8	4'4" 58'7"	3'7" INF	2'11" INF	2'4" INF	1'10" INF	1'4" INF	1'0" INF	0'9" INF	0'7" INF
9	4'7" INF	3'9" INF	3'1" INF	2'5" INF	1'10" INF	1'4" INF	1'1" INF	0'9" INF	0'7" INF
10	4'10" INF	3'11" INF	3'2" INF	2'5" INF	1'11" INF	1'5" INF	1'1" INF	0'9" INF	0'7" INF
12	5'3" INF	4'2" INF	3'4" INF	2'7" INF	1'11" INF	1'5" INF	1'1" INF	0'9" INF	0'7" INF
14	5'7" INF	4'5" INF	3'6" INF	2'8" INF	2'0" INF	1'5" IN	1'1" INF	0'9" INF	0'7" INF
16	5'10" INF	4'7" INF	3'7" INF	2'8" INF	2'0" INF	1'6" INF	1'1" INF	0'9" INF	0'7" INF
18	6'1" INF	4'9" INF	3'8" INF	2'9" INF	2'1" INF	1'6" INF	1'1" INF	0'9" INF	0'7" INF
20	6'4" INF	4'11" INF	3'9" INF	2'9" INF	2'1" INF	1'6" INF	1'1" INF	0'9" INF	0'7" INF
25	6'9" INF	5'2" INF	3'11" INF	2'10" INF	2'1" INF	1'6" INF	1'1" INF	0'9" INF	0'7" INF
50	7'10" INF	5'9" INF	4'3" INF	3'0" INF	2'2" INF	1'7" INF	1'2" INF	0'10" INF	0'7" INF

For circle of confusion = .0005 use depth data two columns left of chosen F-Stop.

16mm — ALL FORMATS DEPTH OF FIELD TABLE — CIRCLE OF CONFUSION=0.0010 inches

FOCUS (focus)	f/1.4 23'7" NEAR	f/1.4 FAR	f/2 16'6" NEAR	f/2 FAR	f/2.8 11'10" NEAR	f/2.8 FAR	f/4 8'3" NEAR	f/4 FAR	f/5.6 5'11" NEAR	f/5.6 FAR	f/8 4'2" NEAR	f/8 FAR	f/11 3'0" NEAR	f/11 FAR	f/16 2'1" NEAR	f/16 FAR	f/22 1'6" NEAR	f/22 FAR
2	1'10"	2'2"	1'9"	2'3"	1'9"	2'5"	1'7"	2'7"	1'6"	3'0"	1'4"	3'9"	1'3"	5'8"	1'0"	INF	0'10"	INF
2½	2'3"	2'9"	2'2"	2'11"	2'1"	3'2"	1'11"	3'7"	1'9"	4'3"	1'7"	6'2"	1'5"	13'5"	1'2"	INF	0'11"	INF
3	2'8"	3'5"	2'7"	3'8"	2'5"	4'0"	2'3"	4'8"	2'0"	6'0"	1'9"	10'5"	1'6"	INF	1'3"	INF	1'0"	INF
3½	3'1"	4'1"	2'11"	4'5"	2'9"	4'11"	2'6"	6'0"	2'3"	8'5"	1'11"	21'1"	1'8"	INF	1'4"	INF	1'1"	INF
4	3'5"	4'10"	3'3"	5'3"	3'0"	6'0"	2'8"	7'8"	2'5"	12'1"	2'1"	INF	1'9"	INF	1'4"	INF	1'1"	INF
4½	3'9"	5'7"	3'7"	6'2"	3'3"	7'3"	2'11"	9'9"	2'7"	18'3"	2'2"	INF	1'10"	INF	1'5"	INF	1'2"	INF
5	4'2"	6'4"	3'10"	7'2"	3'6"	8'7"	3'2"	12'5"	2'9"	30'10"	2'3"	INF	1'11"	INF	1'6"	INF	1'2"	INF
5½	4'6"	7'2"	4'2"	8'2"	3'9"	10'3"	3'4"	16'2"	2'10"	INF	2'4"	INF	1'11"	INF	1'6"	INF	1'2"	INF
6	4'10"	8'0"	4'5"	9'4"	4'0"	12'1"	3'6"	21'5"	3'0"	INF	2'6"	INF	2'0"	INF	1'7"	INF	1'3"	INF

Hyperf. Dist.: f/1.4 = 23'7", f/2 = 16'6", f/2.8 = 11'10", f/4 = 8'3", f/5.6 = 5'11", f/8 = 4'2", f/11 = 3'0", f/16 = 2'1", f/22 = 1'6"

6½	5'1" 8'11"	4'8" 10'8"	4'2" 14'4"	3'8" 29'6"	3'1" INF	2'6" INF	2'1" INF	1'7" INF	1'3" INF
7	5'5" 9'11"	4'11" 12'1"	4'5" 17'0"	3'10" 43'10"	3'3" INF	2'7" INF	2'1" INF	1'7" INF	1'3" INF
8	6'0" 12'1"	5'5" 15'5"	4'9" 24'6"	4'1" INF	3'5" INF	2'9" INF	2'2" INF	1'8" INF	1'3" INF
9	6'6" 14'6"	5'10" 19'7"	5'1" 37'2"	4'4" INF	3'7" INF	2'10" INF	2'3" INF	1'8" INF	1'4" INF
10	7'0" 17'3"	6'3" 25'1"	5'5" 63'5"	4'6" INF	3'9" INF	2'11" INF	2'4" INF	1'9" INF	1'4" INF
12	8'0" 24'3"	7'0" 43'3"	6'0" INF	4'11" INF	4'0" INF	3'1" INF	2'5" INF	1'9" INF	1'4" INF
14	8'10" 34'2"	7'7" 89'6"	6'5" INF	5'3" INF	4'2" INF	3'2" INF	2'6" INF	1'10" INF	1'4" INF
16	9'7" 49'3"	8'2" INF	6'10" INF	5'6" INF	4'4" INF	3'4" INF	2'6" INF	1'10" INF	1'5" INF
18	10'3" 75'0"	8'8" INF	7'2" INF	5'8" INF	4'5" INF	3'4" INF	2'7" INF	1'10" INF	1'5" INF
20	10'10" 128'8"	9'1" INF	7'5" INF	5'10" INF	4'7" INF	3'5" INF	2'7" INF	1'11" INF	1'5" INF
25	12'2" INF	10'0" INF	8'0" INF	6'3" INF	4'9" INF	3'7" INF	2'8" INF	1'11" INF	1'5" INF
50	16'1" INF	12'5" INF	9'7" INF	7'1" INF	5'3" INF	3'10" INF	2'10" INF	2'0" INF	1'6" INF

For circle of confusion = .0005 use depth data two columns left of chosen F-Stop.

18mm — ALL FORMATS DEPTH OF FIELD TABLE — CIRCLE OF CONFUSION=0.0010 inches

FOCUS (feet)		f/1.4	f/2	f/2.8	f/4	f/5.6	f/8	f/11	f/16	f/22
Hyper. Dist.		29' 11"	20' 11"	14' 11"	10' 6"	7' 6"	5' 3"	3' 10"	2' 7"	1' 11"
2	NEAR	1' 11"	1' 10"	1' 9"	1' 8"	1' 7"	1' 6"	1' 4"	1' 2"	1' 0"
	FAR	2' 2"	2' 2"	2' 4"	2' 5"	2' 8"	3' 2"	4' 1"	7' 9"	INF
2½	NEAR	2' 4"	2' 3"	2' 2"	2' 0"	1' 11"	1' 8"	1' 6"	1' 4"	1' 1"
	FAR	2' 9"	2' 10"	3' 0"	3' 3"	3' 9"	4' 8"	7' 0"	INF	INF
3	NEAR	2' 9"	2' 8"	2' 6"	2' 4"	2' 2"	1' 11"	1' 8"	1' 5"	1' 2"
	FAR	3' 4"	3' 6"	3' 9"	4' 2"	4' 11"	6' 10"	13' 3"	INF	INF
3½	NEAR	3' 2"	3' 0"	2' 10"	2' 8"	2' 5"	2' 1"	1' 10"	1' 6"	1' 3"
	FAR	3' 11"	4' 2"	4' 7"	5' 3"	6' 6"	10' 3"	INF	INF	INF
4	NEAR	3' 6"	3' 4"	3' 2"	2' 11"	2' 7"	2' 3"	2' 0"	1' 7"	1' 4"
	FAR	4' 7"	4' 11"	5' 5"	6' 5"	8' 6"	16' 3"	INF	INF	INF
4½	NEAR	3' 11"	3' 9"	3' 6"	3' 2"	2' 10"	2' 5"	2' 1"	1' 8"	1' 4"
	FAR	5' 3"	5' 9"	6' 5"	7' 10"	11' 1"	29' 9"	INF	INF	INF
5	NEAR	4' 3"	4' 1"	3' 9"	3' 5"	3' 0"	2' 7"	2' 2"	1' 9"	1' 5"
	FAR	6' 0"	6' 7"	7' 6"	9' 6"	14' 9"	INF	INF	INF	INF
5½	NEAR	4' 8"	4' 4"	4' 0"	3' 7"	3' 2"	2' 8"	2' 3"	1' 9"	1' 5"
	FAR	6' 9"	7' 5"	8' 8"	11' 6"	20' 3"	INF	INF	INF	INF
6	NEAR	5' 0"	4' 8"	4' 4"	3' 10"	3' 4"	2' 10"	2' 4"	1' 10"	1' 5"
	FAR	7' 6"	8' 5"	9' 11"	13' 11"	29' 3"	INF	INF	INF	INF

f-stop									
6½	5'4" 8'3"	5'0" 9'5"	4'7" 11'5"	4'0" 16'11"	3'6" INF	2'11" INF	2'5" INF	1'11" INF	1'6" INF
7	5'8" 9'1"	5'3" 10'6"	4'9" 13'1"	4'2" 20'10"	3'8" INF	3'0" INF	2'6" INF	1'11" INF	1'6" INF
8	6'4" 10'11"	5'10" 12'11"	5'3" 17'1"	4'7" 33'2"	3'11" INF	3'2" INF	2'7" INF	2'0" INF	1'7" INF
9	6'11" 12'10"	6'4" 15'9"	5'8" 22'5"	4'10" 61'11"	4'1" INF	3'4" INF	2'8" INF	2'0" INF	1'7" INF
10	7'6" 15'0"	6'9" 19'1"	6'0" 29'10"	5'2" INF	4'3" INF	3'5" INF	2'9" INF	2'1" INF	1'7" INF
12	8'7" 20'0"	7'8" 27'11"	6'8" 59'8"	5'7" INF	4'7" INF	3'8" INF	2'11" INF	2'2" INF	1'8" INF
14	9'7" 26'3"	8'5" 41'11"	7'3" INF	6'0" INF	4'11" INF	3'10" INF	3'0" INF	2'3" INF	1'8" INF
16	10'5" 34'3"	9'1" 67'2"	7'9" INF	6'4" INF	5'1" INF	3'11" INF	3'1" INF	2'3" INF	1'8" INF
18	11'3" 45'0"	9'8" 126'3"	8'2" INF	6'8" INF	5'4" INF	4'1" INF	3'2" INF	2'3" INF	1'9" INF
20	12'0" 60'1"	10'3" INF	8'7" INF	6'11" INF	5'5" INF	4'2" INF	3'2" INF	2'4" INF	1'9" INF
25	13'8" 150'11"	11'5" INF	9'4" INF	7'5" INF	5'9" INF	4'4" INF	3'4" INF	2'4" INF	1'9" INF
50	18'9" INF	14'9" INF	11'6" INF	8'8" INF	6'6" INF	4'9" INF	3'6" INF	2'6" INF	1'10" INF

For circle of confusion = .0005 use depth data two columns left of chosen F-Stop.

25mm — ALL FORMATS DEPTH OF FIELD TABLE — CIRCLE OF CONFUSION=0.0010 inches

FOCUS (feet)	f/1.4 NEAR	f/1.4 FAR	f/2 NEAR	f/2 FAR	f/2.8 NEAR	f/2.8 FAR	f/4 NEAR	f/4 FAR	f/5.6 NEAR	f/5.6 FAR	f/8 NEAR	f/8 FAR	f/11 NEAR	f/11 FAR	f/16 NEAR	f/16 FAR	f/22 NEAR	f/22 FAR
Hyper. Dist.	57' 8"		40' 4"		28' 10"		20' 2"		14' 5"		10' 1"		7' 4"		5' 1"		3' 8"	
2	1'11"	2'1"	1'11"	2'1"	1'11"	2'2"	1'10"	2'3"	1'9"	2'4"	1'8"	2'6"	1'7"	2'8"	1'5"	3'3"	1'4"	4'2"
2½	2'5"	2'7"	2'4"	2'8"	2'4"	2'9"	2'3"	2'10"	2'2"	3'0"	2'0"	3'3"	1'11"	3'9"	1'8"	4'10"	1'6"	7'4"
3	2'10"	3'2"	2'10"	3'3"	2'9"	3'4"	2'7"	3'6"	2'6"	3'9"	2'4"	4'3"	2'2"	5'0"	1'11"	7'1"	1'8"	14'8"
3½	3'4"	3'9"	3'3"	3'10"	3'2"	4'0"	3'0"	4'3"	2'10"	4'7"	2'7"	5'4"	2'5"	6'7"	2'1"	10'10"	1'10"	INF
4	3'9"	4'3"	3'8"	4'5"	3'6"	4'8"	3'4"	5'0"	3'2"	5'6"	2'11"	6'6"	2'7"	8'7"	2'3"	17'11"	1'11"	INF
4½	4'2"	4'10"	4'1"	5'1"	3'11"	5'4"	3'8"	5'9"	3'5"	6'6"	3'2"	8'0"	2'10"	11'4"	2'5"	INF	2'1"	INF
5	4'7"	5'6"	4'5"	5'8"	4'3"	6'0"	4'0"	6'7"	3'9"	7'7"	3'4"	9'9"	3'0"	15'2"	2'6"	INF	2'2"	INF
5½	5'0"	6'1"	4'10"	6'4"	4'8"	6'9"	4'4"	7'6"	4'0"	8'10"	3'7"	11'11"	3'2"	21'0"	2'8"	INF	2'3"	INF
6	5'5"	6'8"	5'3"	7'0"	5'0"	7'7"	4'8"	8'6"	4'3"	10'2"	3'9"	14'6"	3'4"	31'0"	2'9"	INF	2'4"	INF

f-stop									
6½	5'10" 7'4"	5'7" 7'9"	5'4" 8'4"	4'11" 9'6"	4'6" 11'9"	4'0" 17'10"	3'6" INF	2'10" INF	2'4" INF
7	6'3" 7'11"	6'0" 8'5"	5'8" 9'3"	5'3" 10'8"	4'9" 13'6"	4'2" 22'3"	3'7" INF	2'11" INF	2'5" INF
8	7'0" 9'3"	6'8" 9'11"	6'3" 11'0"	5'9" 13'2"	5'2" 17'9"	4'6" 37'2"	3'10" INF	3'1" INF	2'6" INF
9	7'10" 10'8"	7'4" 11'7"	6'10" 13'0"	6'3" 16'2"	5'7" 23'7"	4'9" INF	4'1" INF	3'3" INF	2'7" INF
10	8'6" 12'1"	8'0" 13'3"	7'5" 15'3"	6'8" 19'8"	5'11" 32'1"	5'1" INF	4'3" INF	3'4" INF	2'8" INF
12	9'11" 15'2"	9'3" 17'0"	8'6" 20'5"	7'7" 29'4"	6'7" 69'3"	5'6" INF	4'7" INF	3'7" INF	2'10" INF
14	11'3" 18'5"	10'5" 21'4"	9'5" 27'1"	8'3" 45'1"	7'1" INF	5'11" INF	4'10" INF	3'9" INF	2'11" INF
16	12'6" 22'1"	11'6" 26'5"	10'4" 35'9"	8'11" 75'9"	7'7" INF	6'2" INF	5'1" INF	3'10" INF	3'0" INF
18	13'9" 26'1"	12'6" 32'4"	11'1" 47'7"	9'6" INF	8'0" INF	6'6" INF	5'3" INF	3'11" INF	3'1" INF
20	14'10" 30'7"	13'5" 39'6"	11'10" 64'8"	10'1" INF	8'5" INF	6'9" INF	5'5" INF	4'1" INF	3'1" INF
25	17'5" 44'0"	15'5" 65'4"	13'5" 184'2"	11'2" INF	9'2" INF	7'2" INF	5'8" INF	4'3" INF	3'3" INF
50	26'10" 372'3"	22'4" INF	18'4" INF	14'5" INF	11'2" INF	8'5" INF	6'5" INF	4'7" INF	3'5" INF

For circle of confusion = .0005 use depth data two columns left of chosen F-Stop.

35mm — ALL FORMATS DEPTH OF FIELD TABLE — CIRCLE OF CONFUSION=0.0010 inches

FOCUS (feet)	f/1.4	f/2	f/2.8	f/4	f/5.6	f/8	f/11	f/16	f/22
Hyper. Dist.	113' 0"	79' 1"	56' 6"	39' 7"	28' 3"	19' 9"	14' 5"	9' 11"	7' 2"
2 NEAR / FAR	2' 0" / 2' 0"	1' 11" / 2' 1"	1' 11" / 2' 1"	1' 11" / 2' 1"	1' 10" / 2' 2"	1' 10" / 2' 3"	1' 9" / 2' 4"	1' 8" / 2' 6"	1' 7" / 2' 9"
2½ NEAR / FAR	2' 5" / 2' 7"	2' 5" / 2' 7"	2' 5" / 2' 7"	2' 4" / 2' 8"	2' 4" / 2' 9"	2' 3" / 2' 10"	2' 2" / 3' 0"	2' 0" / 3' 4"	1' 11" / 3' 9"
3 NEAR / FAR	2' 11" / 3' 1"	2' 11" / 3' 1"	2' 10" / 3' 2"	2' 10" / 3' 3"	2' 9" / 3' 4"	2' 7" / 3' 6"	2' 6" / 3' 9"	2' 4" / 4' 3"	2' 2" / 5' 0"
3½ NEAR / FAR	3' 5" / 3' 7"	3' 4" / 3' 8"	3' 4" / 3' 9"	3' 3" / 3' 10"	3' 2" / 4' 0"	3' 0" / 4' 3"	2' 10" / 4' 7"	2' 7" / 5' 4"	2' 5" / 6' 7"
4 NEAR / FAR	3' 10" / 4' 2"	3' 10" / 4' 2"	3' 9" / 4' 4"	3' 8" / 4' 5"	3' 6" / 4' 8"	3' 4" / 5' 0"	3' 2" / 5' 6"	2' 10" / 6' 7"	2' 7" / 8' 8"
4½ NEAR / FAR	4' 4" / 4' 8"	4' 3" / 4' 9"	4' 2" / 4' 11"	4' 1" / 5' 1"	3' 11" / 5' 4"	3' 8" / 5' 9"	3' 5" / 6' 6"	3' 1" / 8' 1"	2' 10" / 11' 6"
5 NEAR / FAR	4' 10" / 5' 3"	4' 9" / 5' 4"	4' 7" / 5' 6"	4' 5" / 5' 8"	4' 3" / 6' 1"	4' 0" / 6' 8"	3' 9" / 7' 7"	3' 4" / 9' 11"	3' 0" / 15' 7"
5½ NEAR / FAR	5' 3" / 5' 9"	5' 2" / 5' 11"	5' 0" / 6' 1"	4' 10" / 6' 4"	4' 7" / 6' 10"	4' 4" / 7' 7"	4' 0" / 8' 9"	3' 7" / 12' 1"	3' 2" / 21' 11"
6 NEAR / FAR	5' 8" / 6' 4"	5' 7" / 6' 6"	5' 5" / 6' 8"	5' 3" / 7' 1"	5' 0" / 7' 7"	4' 7" / 8' 6"	4' 3" / 10' 2"	3' 9" / 14' 10"	3' 4" / 33' 0"

6½	6'2" 6'11"	6'0" 7'1"	5'10" 7'4"	5'7" 7'9"	5'4" 8'5"	4'11" 9'7"	4'6" 11'8"	3'11" 18'4"	3'5" INF
7	6'7" 7'5"	6'5" 7'8"	6'3" 8'0"	6'0" 8'6"	5'8" 9'3"	5'2" 10'9"	4'9" 13'5"	4'2" 23'1"	3'7" INF
8	7'6" 8'7"	7'3" 8'11"	7'0" 9'4"	6'8" 10'0"	6'3" 11'1"	5'9" 13'4"	5'2" 17'8"	4'5" 39'6"	3'10" INF
9	8'4" 9'9"	8'1" 10'2"	7'9" 10'8"	7'4" 11'7"	6'10" 13'2"	6'3" 16'4"	5'7" 23'6"	4'9" INF	4'0" INF
10	9'2" 11'0"	8'11" 11'5"	8'6" 12'1"	8'0" 13'4"	7'5" 15'5"	6'8" 20'0"	5'11" 32'0"	5'0" INF	4'3" INF
12	10'10" 13'5"	10'5" 14'1"	9'11" 15'2"	9'3" 17'2"	8'5" 20'9"	7'6" 30'1"	6'7" 69'1"	5'5" INF	4'6" INF
14	12'6" 16'0"	11'11" 17'0"	11'3" 18'7"	10'4" 21'7"	9'5" 27'6"	8'3" 47'0"	7'1" INF	5'10" INF	4'9" INF
16	14'0" 18'7"	13'4" 20'0"	12'6" 22'3"	11'5" 26'9"	10'3" 36'7"	8'10" 81'3"	7'7" INF	6'2" INF	5'0" INF
18	15'6" 21'5"	14'8" 23'3"	13'8" 26'4"	12'5" 32'10"	11'0" 49'1"	9'5" INF	8'0" INF	6'5" INF	5'2" INF
20	17'0" 24'3"	16'0" 26'9"	14'10" 30'10"	13'4" 40'3"	11'9" 67'6"	10'0" INF	8'5" INF	6'8" INF	5'4" INF
25	20'6" 32'1"	19'0" 36'6"	17'4" 44'8"	15'4" 67'5"	13'4" INF	11'1" INF	9'2" INF	7'1" INF	5'7" INF
50	34'8" 89'6"	30'8" 135'4"	26'7" INF	22'1" INF	18'1" INF	14'2" INF	11'2" INF	8'3" INF	6'4" INF

For circle of confusion = .0005 use depth data two columns left of chosen F-Stop.

50mm — ALL FORMATS DEPTH OF FIELD TABLE — CIRCLE OF CONFUSION=0.0010 inches

FOCUS (feet)	f/1.4 NEAR/FAR	f/2 NEAR/FAR	f/2.8 NEAR/FAR	f/4 NEAR/FAR	f/5.6 NEAR/FAR	f/8 NEAR/FAR	f/11 NEAR/FAR	f/16 NEAR/FAR	f/22 NEAR/FAR
Hyper. Dist.	230' 8"	161' 6"	115' 4"	80' 9"	57' 8"	40' 4"	29' 4"	20' 2"	14' 8"
2	2' 0" / 2' 0"	2' 0" / 2' 0"	2' 0" / 2' 0"	1' 11" / 2' 1"	1' 11" / 2' 1"	1' 11" / 2' 1"	1' 11" / 2' 2"	1' 10" / 2' 2"	1' 9" / 2' 3"
2½	2' 6" / 2' 6"	2' 6" / 2' 6"	2' 5" / 2' 7"	2' 5" / 2' 7"	2' 5" / 2' 7"	2' 4" / 2' 8"	2' 4" / 2' 9"	2' 3" / 2' 10"	2' 2" / 3' 0"
3	3' 0" / 3' 0"	2' 11" / 3' 1"	2' 11" / 3' 1"	2' 11" / 3' 1"	2' 10" / 3' 2"	2' 10" / 3' 3"	2' 9" / 3' 4"	2' 8" / 3' 6"	2' 6" / 3' 9"
3½	3' 5" / 3' 7"	3' 5" / 3' 7"	3' 5" / 3' 7"	3' 4" / 3' 8"	3' 4" / 3' 9"	3' 3" / 3' 10"	3' 2" / 3' 11"	3' 0" / 4' 2"	2' 10" / 4' 6"
4	3' 11" / 4' 1"	3' 11" / 4' 1"	3' 10" / 4' 2"	3' 10" / 4' 2"	3' 9" / 4' 3"	3' 8" / 4' 5"	3' 6" / 4' 7"	3' 4" / 4' 11"	3' 2" / 5' 5"
4½	4' 5" / 4' 7"	4' 5" / 4' 7"	4' 4" / 4' 8"	4' 3" / 4' 9"	4' 2" / 4' 10"	4' 1" / 5' 0"	3' 11" / 5' 3"	3' 8" / 5' 9"	3' 6" / 6' 5"
5	4' 11" / 5' 1"	4' 10" / 5' 2"	4' 10" / 5' 3"	4' 9" / 5' 4"	4' 7" / 5' 5"	4' 6" / 5' 8"	4' 4" / 6' 0"	4' 0" / 6' 7"	3' 9" / 7' 5"
5½	5' 5" / 5' 8"	5' 4" / 5' 8"	5' 3" / 5' 9"	5' 2" / 5' 11"	5' 0" / 6' 1"	4' 10" / 6' 4"	4' 8" / 6' 9"	4' 4" / 7' 6"	4' 0" / 8' 8"
6	5' 10" / 6' 2"	5' 9" / 6' 3"	5' 9" / 6' 4"	5' 7" / 6' 6"	5' 5" / 6' 8"	5' 3" / 7' 0"	5' 0" / 7' 6"	4' 8" / 8' 5"	4' 4" / 10' 0"

6½	6'4" 6'8"	6'3" 6'9"	6'2" 6'11"	6'0" 7'1"	5'10" 7'4"	5'7" 7'9"	5'4" 8'3"	4'11" 9'6"	4'6" 11'5"
7	6'10" 7'3"	6'9" 7'4"	6'7" 7'5"	6'5" 7'8"	6'3" 7'11"	6'0" 8'5"	5'8" 9'1"	5'3" 10'7"	4'9" 13'1"
8	7'9" 8'3"	7'8" 8'5"	7'6" 8'7"	7'4" 8'10"	7'1" 9'3"	6'8" 9'11"	6'4" 10'11"	5'9" 13'1"	5'3" 17'2"
9	8'8" 9'4"	8'6" 9'6"	8'4" 9'9"	8'1" 10'1"	7'10" 10'8"	7'5" 11'6"	6'11" 12'11"	6'3" 16'0"	5'7" 22'7"
10	9'7" 10'5"	9'5" 10'8"	9'3" 10'11"	8'11" 11'5"	8'7" 12'1"	8'0" 13'3"	7'6" 15'0"	6'9" 19'6"	6'0" 30'4"
12	11'5" 12'8"	11'2" 12'11"	10'11" 13'4"	10'6" 14'1"	9'11" 15'1"	9'3" 17'0"	8'7" 20'1"	7'7" 29'0"	6'8" 62'0"
14	13'2" 14'11"	12'11" 15'4"	12'6" 15'11"	11'11" 16'11"	11'3" 18'5"	10'5" 21'4"	9'6" 26'6"	8'4" 44'6"	7'2" INF
16	15'0" 17'2"	14'7" 17'9"	14'1" 18'7"	13'5" 19'11"	12'7" 22'1"	11'6" 26'4"	10'5" 34'9"	9'0" 74'4"	7'8" INF
18	16'8" 19'6"	16'3" 20'3"	15'7" 21'4"	14'9" 23'1"	13'9" 26'1"	12'6" 32'3"	11'2" 45'10"	9'7" INF	8'2" INF
20	18'5" 21'11"	17'10" 22'10"	17'1" 24'2"	16'1" 26'6"	14'11" 30'6"	13'5" 39'4"	11'11" 61'8"	10'1" INF	8'6" INF
25	22'7" 28'0"	21'8" 29'7"	20'7" 31'10"	19'1" 36'1"	17'6" 43'11"	15'6" 65'0"	13'7" 162'4"	11'2" INF	9'3" INF
50	41'1" 63'9"	38'2" 72'4"	34'11" 88'1"	30'11" 130'8"	26'10" 368'4"	22'4" INF	18'6" INF	14'5" INF	11'5" INF

For circle of confusion = .0005 use depth data two columns left of chosen F-Stop.

85mm — ALL FORMATS DEPTH OF FIELD TABLE — CIRCLE OF CONFUSION=0.0010 inches

	f/1.4		f/2		f/2.8		f/4		f/5.6		f/8		f/11		f/16		f/22	
Hyper. Dist.	666' 7"		466' 7"		333' 4"		233' 4"		166' 8"		116' 8"		84' 10"		58' 4"		42' 5"	
FOCUS (feet)	NEAR	FAR	NEAR	FAR	NEAR	FAR	NEAR	FAR	NEAR	FAR	NEAR	FAR	NEAR	FAR	NEAR	FAR	NEAR	FAR
2	2' 0"	2' 0"	2' 0"	2' 0"	2' 0"	2' 0"	2' 0"	2' 0"	2' 0"	2' 0"	2' 0"	2' 0"	2' 0"	2' 0"	1' 11"	2' 1"	1' 11"	2' 1"
2½	2' 6"	2' 6"	2' 6"	2' 6"	2' 6"	2' 6"	2' 6"	2' 6"	2' 6"	2' 6"	2' 5"	2' 7"	2' 5"	2' 7"	2' 5"	2' 7"	2' 5"	2' 8"
3	3' 0"	3' 0"	3' 0"	3' 0"	3' 0"	3' 0"	3' 0"	3' 0"	2' 11"	3' 1"	2' 11"	3' 1"	2' 11"	3' 1"	2' 10"	3' 2"	2' 10"	3' 2"
3½	3' 6"	3' 6"	3' 6"	3' 6"	3' 6"	3' 6"	3' 5"	3' 7"	3' 5"	3' 7"	3' 5"	3' 7"	3' 4"	3' 8"	3' 4"	3' 8"	3' 3"	3' 9"
4	4' 0"	4' 0"	4' 0"	4' 0"	3' 11"	4' 1"	3' 11"	4' 1"	3' 11"	4' 1"	3' 11"	4' 2"	3' 10"	4' 2"	3' 9"	4' 3"	3' 8"	4' 5"
4½	4' 6"	4' 6"	4' 6"	4' 6"	4' 5"	4' 7"	4' 5"	4' 7"	4' 5"	4' 7"	4' 4"	4' 8"	4' 3"	4' 9"	4' 2"	4' 10"	4' 1"	5' 0"
5	5' 0"	5' 0"	4' 11"	5' 1"	4' 11"	5' 1"	4' 11"	5' 1"	4' 10"	5' 2"	4' 10"	5' 3"	4' 9"	5' 4"	4' 8"	5' 5"	4' 6"	5' 8"
5½	5' 5"	5' 7"	5' 5"	5' 7"	5' 5"	5' 7"	5' 5"	5' 8"	5' 4"	5' 8"	5' 3"	5' 9"	5' 2"	5' 10"	5' 1"	6' 0"	4' 11"	6' 3"
6	5' 11"	6' 1"	5' 11"	6' 1"	5' 11"	6' 1"	5' 10"	6' 2"	5' 10"	6' 3"	5' 9"	6' 4"	5' 7"	6' 5"	5' 6"	6' 8"	5' 3"	6' 11"

6½	6' 5" 6' 7"	6' 5" 6' 7"	6' 5" 6' 7"	6' 4" 6' 8"	6' 3" 6' 9"	6' 2" 6' 10"	6' 1" 7' 0"	5' 10" 7' 3"	5' 8" 7' 7"
7	6' 11" 7' 1"	6' 11" 7' 1"	6' 10" 7' 2"	6' 10" 7' 2"	6' 9" 7' 4"	6' 7" 7' 5"	6' 6" 7' 7"	6' 3" 7' 11"	6' 1" 8' 4"
8	7' 11" 8' 1"	7' 10" 8' 2"	7' 10" 8' 2"	7' 9" 8' 3"	7' 8" 8' 5"	7' 6" 8' 7"	7' 4" 8' 10"	7' 1" 9' 3"	6' 9" 9' 9"
9	8' 11" 9' 1"	8' 10" 9' 2"	8' 9" 9' 3"	8' 8" 9' 4"	8' 7" 9' 6"	8' 4" 9' 9"	8' 2" 10' 0"	7' 10" 10' 7"	7' 6" 11' 4"
10	9' 10" 10' 2"	9' 10" 10' 3"	9' 9" 10' 4"	9' 7" 10' 5"	9' 5" 10' 7"	9' 3" 10' 11"	9' 0" 11' 4"	8' 7" 12' 0"	8' 2" 13' 0"
12	11' 10" 12' 3"	11' 8" 12' 4"	11' 7" 12' 5"	11' 5" 12' 8"	11' 3" 12' 11"	10' 11" 13' 4"	10' 7" 13' 11"	10' 0" 15' 0"	9' 5" 16' 7"
14	13' 9" 14' 4"	13' 7" 14' 5"	13' 5" 14' 7"	13' 3" 14' 10"	12' 11" 15' 3"	12' 6" 15' 10"	12' 1" 16' 8"	11' 4" 18' 4"	10' 7" 20' 8"
16	15' 8" 16' 5"	15' 6" 16' 7"	15' 3" 16' 10"	15' 0" 17' 2"	14' 7" 17' 8"	14' 1" 18' 6"	13' 6" 19' 8"	12' 7" 21' 11"	11' 8" 25' 5"
18	17' 6" 18' 6"	17' 4" 18' 9"	17' 1" 19' 0"	16' 9" 19' 6"	16' 3" 20' 2"	15' 8" 21' 3"	14' 11" 22' 9"	13' 10" 25' 10"	12' 8" 30' 11"
20	19' 5" 20' 7"	19' 2" 20' 11"	18' 11" 21' 3"	18' 5" 21' 10"	17' 11" 22' 8"	17' 1" 24' 1"	16' 3" 26' 1"	14' 11" 30' 3"	13' 8" 37' 5"
25	24' 1" 26' 0"	23' 9" 26' 5"	23' 3" 27' 0"	22' 7" 28' 0"	21' 9" 29' 4"	20' 8" 31' 9"	19' 4" 35' 3"	17' 7" 43' 5"	15' 10" 59' 11"
50	46' 6" 54' 0"	45' 2" 56' 0"	43' 6" 58' 9"	41' 3" 63' 6"	38' 6" 71' 3"	35' 1" 87' 2"	31' 6" 120' 9"	27' 0" 338' 11"	23' 0" INF

For circle of confusion = .0005 use depth data two columns left of chosen F-Stop.

100mm　　ALL FORMATS DEPTH OF FIELD TABLE　　CIRCLE OF CONFUSION=0.0010 inches

	f/1.4	f/2	f/2.8	f/4	f/5.6	f/8	f/11	f/16	f/22
Hyper. Dist.	INF	645' 10"	461' 4"	322' 11"	230' 8"	161' 6"	117' 5"	80' 9"	58' 9"
FOCUS (feet)	NEAR FAR	NEAR FAR	NEAR FAR	NEAR FAR	NEAR FAR	NEAR FAR	NEAR FAR	NEAR FAR	NEAR FAR
2	2' 0" 2' 0"	2' 0" 2' 0"	2' 0" 2' 0"	2' 0" 2' 0"	2' 0" 2' 0"	2' 0" 2' 0"	2' 0" 2' 0"	2' 0" 2' 1"	1' 11" 2' 1"
2½	2' 6" 2' 6"	2' 6" 2' 6"	2' 6" 2' 6"	2' 6" 2' 6"	2' 6" 2' 6"	2' 6" 2' 6"	2' 5" 2' 7"	2' 5" 2' 7"	2' 5" 2' 7"
3	3' 0" 3' 0"	3' 0" 3' 0"	3' 0" 3' 0"	3' 0" 3' 0"	3' 0" 3' 0"	2' 11" 3' 1"	2' 11" 3' 1"	2' 11" 3' 1"	2' 10" 3' 2"
3½	3' 6" 3' 6"	3' 6" 3' 6"	3' 6" 3' 6"	3' 6" 3' 6"	3' 5" 3' 7"	3' 5" 3' 7"	3' 5" 3' 7"	3' 4" 3' 8"	3' 4" 3' 8"
4	4' 0" 4' 0"	4' 0" 4' 0"	4' 0" 4' 0"	3' 11" 4' 1"	3' 11" 4' 1"	3' 11" 4' 1"	3' 11" 4' 2"	3' 10" 4' 2"	3' 9" 4' 3"
4½	4' 6" 4' 6"	4' 6" 4' 6"	4' 6" 4' 6"	4' 5" 4' 7"	4' 5" 4' 7"	4' 5" 4' 7"	4' 4" 4' 8"	4' 3" 4' 9"	4' 2" 4' 10"
5	5' 0" 5' 0"	5' 0" 5' 0"	4' 11" 5' 1"	4' 11" 5' 1"	4' 11" 5' 1"	4' 10" 5' 2"	4' 10" 5' 2"	4' 9" 5' 4"	4' 8" 5' 5"
5½	5' 5" 5' 6"	5' 5" 5' 7"	5' 5" 5' 7"	5' 5" 5' 7"	5' 5" 5' 8"	5' 4" 5' 8"	5' 3" 5' 9"	5' 2" 5' 11"	5' 1" 6' 0"
6	6' 0" 6' 0"	5' 11" 6' 1"	5' 11" 6' 1"	5' 11" 6' 1"	5' 10" 6' 2"	5' 10" 6' 3"	5' 9" 6' 4"	5' 7" 6' 5"	5' 6" 6' 8"

f	1	2	3	4	5	6	7	8	9
6½	6'5" / 6'7"	6'5" / 6'7"	6'5" / 6'7"	6'5" / 6'8"	6'4" / 6'8"	6'3" / 6'9"	6'2" / 6'10"	6'0" / 7'0"	5'11" / 7'3"
7	6'11" / 7'1"	6'11" / 7'1"	6'11" / 7'1"	6'10" / 7'2"	6'10" / 7'3"	6'9" / 7'4"	6'7" / 7'5"	6'6" / 7'8"	6'3" / 7'11"
8	7'11" / 8'1"	7'11" / 8'1"	7'10" / 8'2"	7'10" / 8'2"	7'9" / 8'3"	7'8" / 8'5"	7'6" / 8'7"	7'4" / 8'10"	7'1" / 9'2"
9	8'11" / 9'1"	8'11" / 9'1"	8'10" / 9'2"	8'9" / 9'3"	8'8" / 9'4"	8'6" / 9'6"	8'5" / 9'9"	8'2" / 10'1"	7'10" / 10'7"
10	9'11" / 10'1"	9'10" / 10'2"	9'10" / 10'3"	9'9" / 10'4"	9'7" / 10'5"	9'5" / 10'8"	9'3" / 10'11"	8'11" / 11'4"	8'7" / 12'0"
12	11'10" / 12'2"	11'9" / 12'3"	11'8" / 12'4"	11'7" / 12'5"	11'5" / 12'8"	11'2" / 12'11"	10'11" / 13'4"	10'6" / 14'0"	10'0" / 15'0"
14	13'10" / 14'3"	13'9" / 14'4"	13'7" / 14'5"	13'5" / 14'7"	13'3" / 14'11"	12'11" / 15'4"	12'6" / 15'10"	12'0" / 16'10"	11'4" / 18'3"
16	15'9" / 16'3"	15'7" / 16'5"	15'6" / 16'7"	15'3" / 16'10"	15'0" / 17'2"	14'7" / 17'9"	14'1" / 18'6"	13'5" / 19'10"	12'8" / 21'10"
18	17'8" / 18'4"	17'6" / 18'6"	17'4" / 18'9"	17'1" / 19'1"	16'9" / 19'6"	16'3" / 20'3"	15'8" / 21'2"	14'9" / 23'1"	13'10" / 25'9"
20	19'7" / 20'5"	19'5" / 20'8"	19'2" / 20'11"	18'10" / 21'4"	18'5" / 21'10"	17'10" / 22'9"	17'2" / 24'0"	16'1" / 26'5"	15'0" / 30'1"
25	24'4" / 25'8"	24'1" / 26'0"	23'9" / 26'5"	23'3" / 27'1"	22'7" / 28'0"	21'8" / 29'6"	20'8" / 31'8"	19'2" / 36'0"	17'7" / 43'1"
50	47'5" / 52'10"	46'5" / 54'2"	45'2" / 56'0"	43'4" / 59'1"	41'2" / 63'9"	38'3" / 72'3"	35'2" / 86'8"	30'11" / 130'0"	27'1" / 324'9"

For circle of confusion = .0005 use depth data two columns left of chosen F-Stop.

200mm — ALL FORMATS DEPTH OF FIELD TABLE — CIRCLE OF CONFUSION=0.0010 inches

FOCUS (feet)	f/1.4 NEAR / FAR	f/2 NEAR / FAR	f/2.8 NEAR / FAR	f/4 NEAR / FAR	f/5.6 NEAR / FAR	f/8 NEAR / FAR	f/11 NEAR / FAR	f/16 NEAR / FAR	f/22 NEAR / FAR
Hyper. Dist.	INF	INF	INF	INF	645' 10"	469' 8"	322' 11"	234' 10"	161' 6"
5	5' 0" / 5' 0"	5' 0" / 5' 0"	5' 0" / 5' 0"	5' 0" / 5' 0"	5' 0" / 5' 0"	4' 11" / 5' 1"	4' 11" / 5' 1"	4' 11" / 5' 1"	4' 10" / 5' 2"
5½	5' 6" / 5' 6"	5' 6" / 5' 6"	5' 6" / 5' 6"	5' 6" / 5' 6"	5' 6" / 5' 6"	5' 5" / 5' 7"	5' 5" / 5' 7"	5' 5" / 5' 7"	5' 4" / 5' 8"
6	6' 0" / 6' 0"	6' 0" / 6' 0"	6' 0" / 6' 0"	6' 0" / 6' 0"	5' 11" / 6' 1"	5' 11" / 6' 1"	5' 11" / 6' 1"	5' 10" / 6' 2"	5' 10" / 6' 2"
6½	6' 6" / 6' 6"	6' 6" / 6' 6"	6' 6" / 6' 6"	6' 6" / 6' 6"	6' 5" / 6' 7"	6' 5" / 6' 7"	6' 5" / 6' 7"	6' 4" / 6' 8"	6' 3" / 6' 9"
7	7' 0" / 7' 0"	7' 0" / 7' 0"	7' 0" / 7' 0"	6' 11" / 7' 1"	6' 11" / 7' 1"	6' 11" / 7' 1"	6' 10" / 7' 2"	6' 10" / 7' 2"	6' 9" / 7' 3"
8	8' 0" / 8' 0"	8' 0" / 8' 0"	7' 11" / 8' 1"	7' 11" / 8' 1"	7' 11" / 8' 1"	7' 11" / 8' 2"	7' 10" / 8' 2"	7' 9" / 8' 3"	7' 8" / 8' 5"
9	9' 0" / 9' 0"	9' 0" / 9' 0"	8' 11" / 9' 1"	8' 11" / 9' 1"	8' 11" / 9' 1"	8' 10" / 9' 2"	8' 9" / 9' 3"	8' 8" / 9' 4"	8' 7" / 9' 6"
10	10' 0" / 10' 0"	9' 11" / 10' 1"	9' 11" / 10' 1"	9' 11" / 10' 1"	9' 10" / 10' 2"	9' 10" / 10' 2"	9' 9" / 10' 4"	9' 7" / 10' 5"	9' 5" / 10' 7"
12	11' 11" / 12' 1"	11' 11" / 12' 1"	11' 11" / 12' 1"	11' 10" / 12' 2"	11' 10" / 12' 3"	11' 9" / 12' 4"	11' 7" / 12' 5"	11' 5" / 12' 7"	11' 3" / 12' 11"

f	1	2	3	4	5	6	7	8	9
14	13'11" / 14'1"	13'11" / 14'1"	13'10" / 14'2"	13'10" / 14'2"	13'9" / 14'4"	13'7" / 14'5"	13'5" / 14'7"	13'3" / 14'10"	12'11" / 15'3"
16	15'11" / 16'1"	15'10" / 16'2"	15'10" / 16'2"	15'9" / 16'3"	15'8" / 16'5"	15'6" / 16'6"	15'0" / 16'10"	15'0" / 17'1"	14'7" / 17'8"
18	17'11" / 18'1"	17'10" / 18'2"	17'9" / 18'3"	17'8" / 18'4"	17'6" / 18'6"	17'4" / 18'8"	17'1" / 19'0"	16'9" / 19'5"	16'3" / 20'2"
20	19'10" / 20'2"	19'10" / 20'3"	19'8" / 20'4"	19'7" / 20'5"	19'5" / 20'7"	19'3" / 20'10"	18'10" / 21'3"	18'6" / 21'10"	17'10" / 22'9"
25	24'9" / 25'3"	24'8" / 25'4"	24'6" / 25'6"	24'4" / 25'8"	24'1" / 26'0"	23'9" / 26'4"	23'3" / 27'0"	22'8" / 27'11"	21'9" / 29'5"
50	49'1" / 51'0"	48'8" / 51'4"	48'2" / 52'0"	47'6" / 52'10"	46'5" / 54'2"	45'3" / 55'10"	43'4" / 59'0"	41'4" / 63'4"	38'4" / 72'0"
75	72'11" / 77'3"	72'1" / 78'2"	70'11" / 79'7"	69'5" / 81'7"	67'3" / 84'9"	64'9" / 89'1"	61'0" / 97'5"	57'0" / 109'9"	51'4" / 139'0"
100	96'4" / 104'0"	94'11" / 105'8"	92'10" / 108'4"	90'3" / 112'1"	86'8" / 118'2"	82'7" / 126'10"	76'6" / 144'5"	70'3" / 173'4"	61'11" / 259'11"
125	119'3" / 131'4"	117'1" / 134'0"	114'0" / 138'4"	110'2" / 144'6"	104'10" / 154'10"	98'10" / 170'0"	90'3" / 203'3"	81'9" / 265'8"	70'7" / 543'9"
150	141'10" / 159'2"	138'8" / 163'3"	134'5" / 169'7"	129'1" / 179'0"	121'10" / 195'1"	113'10" / 219'11"	102'7" / 279'1"	91'8" / 412'0"	77'11" / INF
175	163'11" / 187'8"	159'11" / 193'3"	154'2" / 202'4"	147'2" / 215'9"	137'10" / 239'9"	127'8" / 278'4"	113'8" / 380'4"	100'5" / 679'3"	84'2" / INF
200	185'8" / 216'9"	180'6" / 224'3"	173'3" / 236'6"	164'6" / 255'1"	152'10" / 289'4"	140'5" / 347'6"	123'8" / 522'8"	108'2" / 1322'11"	89'6" / INF

For circle of confusion = .0005 use depth data two columns left of chosen F-Stop.

10mm FIELD OF VIEW

SETUPS (Approximate Distance)

	Full Aperture V 86.1° H 102.4°	Academy 1.33:1 V 74.8° H 97.7°	Academy 1.66:1 V 64.5° H 92.7°	Academy 1.85:1 V 59.1° H 92.1°	Anamorphic 2.40:1	Super 35 1.85:1 V 66.0° H 100.4°	Super 35 2.40:1 V 53.2° H 100.4°
Ext Close Up	0' 5"	0' 6"	0' 7"	0' 8"	NA	0' 7"	0' 9"
Close Up	0' 7"	0' 9"	0' 11"	1' 0"	NA	0' 11"	1' 2"
Medium Shot	1' 2"	1' 4"	1' 8"	1' 10"	NA	1' 8"	2' 0"
Full Figure	3' 3"	3' 9"	4' 6"	5' 1"	NA	4' 7"	6' 0"

Angle of View

Angle of View	Full Aperture	Academy 1.33:1	Academy 1.66:1	Academy 1.85:1	Anamorphic 2.40:1	Super 35 1.85:1	Super 35 2.40:1	VistaVision	VistaVision 1.85:1	VistaVision 2.40:1	65mm
2	3' 9" 5' 0"	3' 2" 4' 5"	2' 8" 4' 5"	2' 5" 4' 5"	NA NA	2' 7" 4' 10"	2' 0" 4' 10"	NA NA	NA NA	NA NA	NA NA
2½	4' 8" 6' 3"	4' 0" 5' 6"	3' 4" 5' 6"	3' 0" 5' 6"	NA NA	3' 3" 6' 0"	2' 6" 6' 0"	NA NA	NA NA	NA NA	NA NA
3	5' 7" 7' 6"	4' 10" 6' 7"	4' 0" 6' 7"	3' 7" 6' 7"	NA NA	3' 11" 7' 2"	3' 0" 7' 2"	NA NA	NA NA	NA NA	NA NA
3½	6' 6" 8' 9"	5' 7" 7' 8"	4' 8" 7' 8"	4' 2" 7' 8"	NA NA	4' 7" 8' 5"	3' 6" 8' 5"	NA NA	NA NA	NA NA	NA NA
4	7' 6" 10' 0"	6' 5" 8' 10"	5' 4" 8' 10"	4' 9" 8' 10"	NA NA	5' 2" 9' 7"	4' 0" 9' 7"	NA NA	NA NA	NA NA	NA NA
4½	8' 5" 11' 3"	7' 3" 9' 11"	6' 0" 9' 11"	5' 4" 9' 11"	NA NA	5' 10" 10' 10"	4' 6" 10' 10"	NA NA	NA NA	NA NA	NA NA
5	9' 4" 12' 6"	8' 0" 11' 0"	6' 8" 11' 0"	5' 11" 11' 0"	NA NA	6' 6" 12' 0"	5' 0" 12' 0"	NA NA	NA NA	NA NA	NA NA
5½	10' 3" 13' 8"	8' 10" 12' 1"	7' 4" 12' 1"	6' 6" 12' 1"	NA NA	7' 2" 13' 2"	5' 6" 13' 2"	NA NA	NA NA	NA NA	NA NA
6	11' 2" 14' 11"	9' 7" 13' 2"	7' 11" 13' 2"	7' 2" 13' 2"	NA NA	7' 9" 14' 5"	6' 0" 14' 5"	NA NA	NA NA	NA NA	NA NA

6½	12'2" / 16'2"	10'5" / 14'4"	8'7" / 14'4"	7'9" / 14'4"	NA / NA	8'5" / 15'7"	6'6" / 15'7"	NA / NA	NA / NA	NA / NA	NA / NA	NA / NA
7	13'1" / 17'5"	11'3" / 15'5"	9'3" / 15'5"	8'4" / 15'5"	NA / NA	9'1" / 16'10"	7'0" / 16'10"	NA / NA	NA / NA	NA / NA	NA / NA	NA / NA
8	14'11" / 19'11"	12'10" / 17'7"	10'7" / 17'7"	9'6" / 17'7"	NA / NA	10'5" / 19'2"	8'0" / 19'2"	NA / NA	NA / NA	NA / NA	NA / NA	NA / NA
9	16'10" / 22'5"	14'5" / 19'10"	11'11" / 19'10"	10'8" / 19'10"	NA / NA	11'8" / 21'7"	9'0" / 21'7"	NA / NA	NA / NA	NA / NA	NA / NA	NA / NA
10	18'8" / 24'11"	16'0" / 22'0"	13'3" / 22'0"	11'11" / 22'0"	NA / NA	13'0" / 24'0"	10'0" / 24'0"	NA / NA	NA / NA	NA / NA	NA / NA	NA / NA
12	22'5" / 29'11"	19'3" / 26'5"	15'11" / 26'5"	14'3" / 26'5"	NA / NA	15'7" / 28'10"	12'0" / 28'10"	NA / NA	NA / NA	NA / NA	NA / NA	NA / NA
14	26'2" / 34'11"	22'5" / 30'10"	18'7" / 30'10"	16'8" / 30'10"	NA / NA	18'2" / 33'7"	14'0" / 33'7"	NA / NA	NA / NA	NA / NA	NA / NA	NA / NA
16	29'10" / 39'10"	25'8" / 35'2"	21'3" / 35'2"	19'0" / 35'2"	NA / NA	20'9" / 38'5"	16'0" / 38'5"	NA / NA	NA / NA	NA / NA	NA / NA	NA / NA
18	33'7" / 44'10"	28'10" / 39'7"	23'10" / 39'7"	21'5" / 39'7"	NA / NA	23'4" / 43'2"	18'0" / 43'2"	NA / NA	NA / NA	NA / NA	NA / NA	NA / NA
20	37'4" / 49'10"	32'1" / 44'0"	26'6" / 44'0"	23'9" / 44'0"	NA / NA	26'0" / 48'0"	20'0" / 48'0"	NA / NA	NA / NA	NA / NA	NA / NA	NA / NA
25	46'8" / 62'4"	40'1" / 55'0"	33'2" / 55'0"	29'9" / 55'0"	NA / NA	32'5" / 60'0"	25'0" / 60'0"	NA / NA	NA / NA	NA / NA	NA / NA	NA / NA
50	93'4" / 124'7"	80'2" / 110'0"	66'4" / 110'0"	59'5" / 110'0"	NA / NA	64'11" / 120'0"	50'0" / 120'0"	NA / NA	NA / NA	NA / NA	NA / NA	NA / NA

SETUPS (Approximate Distance) — 16mm FIELD OF VIEW

	Full Aperture	Academy 1.33:1	Academy 1.66:1	Academy 1.85:1	Anamorphic 2.40:1	Super 35 1.85:1	Super 35 2.40:1	VistaVision	VistaVision 1.85:1	VistaVision 2.40:1	65mm
Ext Close Up	0' 8"	0' 9"	0' 11"	1' 0"	NA	0' 11"	1' 2"	NA	NA	NA	NA
Close Up	1' 0"	1' 2"	1' 5"	1' 7"	NA	1' 5"	1' 10"	NA	NA	NA	NA
Medium Shot	1' 10"	2' 2"	2' 7"	2' 11"	NA	2' 8"	3' 6"	NA	NA	NA	NA
Full Figure	5' 2"	6' 0"	7' 3"	8' 1"	NA	7' 5"	9' 7"	NA	NA	NA	NA
Angle of View	V 60.5° H 75.8°	V 51.1° H 66.4°	V 43.1° H 66.4°	V 39.0° H 66.4°	NA NA	V 44.2° H 73.7°	V 34.7° H 73.7°	NA NA	NA NA	NA NA	NA NA
2	2' 4" / 3' 1"	2' 0" / 2' 9"	1' 8" / 2' 9"	1' 6" / 2' 9"	NA NA	1' 7" / 3' 0"	1' 3" / 3' 0"	NA NA	NA NA	NA NA	NA NA
2½	2' 11" / 3' 11"	2' 6" / 3' 5"	2' 1" / 3' 5"	1' 10" / 3' 5"	NA NA	2' 0" / 3' 9"	1' 7" / 3' 9"	NA NA	NA NA	NA NA	NA NA
3	3' 6" / 4' 8"	3' 0" / 4' 1"	2' 6" / 4' 1"	2' 3" / 4' 1"	NA NA	2' 5" / 4' 6"	1' 11" / 4' 6"	NA NA	NA NA	NA NA	NA NA
3½	4' 1" / 5' 5"	3' 6" / 4' 10"	2' 11" / 4' 10"	2' 7" / 4' 10"	NA NA	2' 10" / 5' 3"	2' 2" / 5' 3"	NA NA	NA NA	NA NA	NA NA
4	4' 8" / 6' 3"	4' 0" / 5' 6"	3' 4" / 5' 6"	3' 0" / 5' 6"	NA NA	3' 3" / 6' 0"	2' 6" / 6' 0"	NA NA	NA NA	NA NA	NA NA
4½	5' 3" / 7' 0"	4' 6" / 6' 2"	3' 9" / 6' 2"	3' 4" / 6' 2"	NA NA	3' 8" / 6' 9"	2' 10" / 6' 9"	NA NA	NA NA	NA NA	NA NA
5	5' 10" / 7' 9"	5' 0" / 6' 10"	4' 2" / 6' 10"	3' 9" / 6' 10"	NA NA	4' 1" / 7' 6"	3' 2" / 7' 6"	NA NA	NA NA	NA NA	NA NA
5½	6' 5" / 8' 7"	5' 6" / 7' 7"	4' 7" / 7' 7"	4' 1" / 7' 7"	NA NA	4' 6" / 8' 3"	3' 5" / 8' 3"	NA NA	NA NA	NA NA	NA NA
6	7' 0" / 9' 4"	6' 0" / 8' 3"	5' 0" / 8' 3"	4' 5" / 8' 3"	NA NA	4' 10" / 9' 0"	3' 9" / 9' 0"	NA NA	NA NA	NA NA	NA NA

6½	7' 7" 10' 1"	6' 6" 8' 11"	5' 5" 8' 11"	4' 10" 8' 11"	NA NA	5' 3" 9' 9"	4' 1" 9' 9"	NA NA	NA NA	NA NA	NA NA
7	8' 2" 10' 11"	7' 0" 9' 7"	5' 10" 9' 7"	5' 2" 9' 7"	NA NA	5' 8" 10' 6"	4' 5" 10' 6"	NA NA	NA NA	NA NA	NA NA
8	9' 4" 12' 6"	8' 0" 11' 0"	6' 8" 11' 0"	5' 11" 11' 0"	NA NA	6' 6" 12' 0"	5' 0" 12' 0"	NA NA	NA NA	NA NA	NA NA
9	10' 6" 14' 0"	9' 0" 12' 4"	7' 5" 12' 4"	6' 8" 12' 4"	NA NA	7' 4" 13' 6"	5' 8" 13' 6"	NA NA	NA NA	NA NA	NA NA
10	11' 8" 15' 7"	10' 0" 13' 9"	8' 3" 13' 9"	7' 5" 13' 9"	NA NA	8' 1" 15' 0"	6' 3" 15' 0"	NA NA	NA NA	NA NA	NA NA
12	14' 0" 18' 8"	12' 0" 16' 6"	9' 11" 16' 6"	8' 11" 16' 6"	NA NA	9' 9" 18' 0"	7' 6" 18' 0"	NA NA	NA NA	NA NA	NA NA
14	16' 4" 21' 10"	14' 0" 19' 3"	11' 7" 19' 3"	10' 5" 19' 3"	NA NA	11' 4" 21' 0"	8' 9" 21' 0"	NA NA	NA NA	NA NA	NA NA
16	18' 8" 24' 11"	16' 0" 22' 0"	13' 3" 22' 0"	11' 11" 22' 0"	NA NA	13' 0" 24' 0"	10' 0" 24' 0"	NA NA	NA NA	NA NA	NA NA
18	21' 0" 28' 0"	18' 0" 24' 9"	14' 11" 24' 9"	13' 4" 24' 9"	NA NA	14' 7" 27' 0"	11' 3" 27' 0"	NA NA	NA NA	NA NA	NA NA
20	23' 4" 31' 2"	20' 0" 27' 6"	16' 7" 27' 6"	14' 10" 27' 6"	NA NA	16' 3" 30' 0"	12' 6" 30' 0"	NA NA	NA NA	NA NA	NA NA
25	29' 2" 38' 11"	25' 1" 34' 4"	20' 9" 34' 4"	18' 7" 34' 4"	NA NA	20' 3" 37' 6"	15' 8" 37' 6"	NA NA	NA NA	NA NA	NA NA
50	58' 4" 77' 10"	50' 1" 68' 9"	41' 5" 68' 9"	37' 2" 68' 9"	NA NA	40' 7" 75' 0"	31' 3" 75' 0"	NA NA	NA NA	NA NA	NA NA

SETUPS (Approximate Distance)

18mm FIELD OF VIEW

Angle of View	Full Aperture V 54.8° H 69.3°	Academy 1.33:1 V 46.0° H 60.4°	Academy 1.66:1 V 38.6° H 60.4°	Academy 1.85:1 V 34.9° H 60.4°	Anamorphic 2.40:1 V 52.6° H 99.6°	Super 35 1.85:1 V 39.7° H 67.4°	Super 35 2.40:1 V 31.1° H 67.4°	VistaVision V 69.9° H 92.7°	VistaVision 1.85:1 V 59.1° H 92.7°	VistaVision 2.40:1 V 47.3° H 92.7°	65mm
Ext Close Up	0'9"	0'10"	1'0"	1'2"	0'9"	1'0"	1'4"	0'7"	0'8"	0'10"	NA
Close Up	1'1"	1'4"	1'7"	1'9"	1'2"	1'7"	2'1"	0'10"	1'0"	1'4"	NA
Medium Shot	2'1"	2'5"	2'11"	3'3"	2'1"	3'0"	3'11"	1'7"	1'11"	2'6"	NA
Full Figure	5'9"	6'9"	8'2"	9'1"	5'10"	8'4"	10'10"	4'4"	5'4"	6'10"	NA
2	2'1" / 2'9"	1'9" / 2'5"	1'6" / 2'5"	1'4" / 2'5"	2'1" / 4'11"	1'5" / 2'8"	1'1" / 2'8"	2'9" / 4'2"	2'3" / 4'2"	1'9" / 4'2"	NA / NA
2½	2'7" / 3'6"	2'3" / 3'1"	1'10" / 3'1"	1'8" / 3'1"	2'7" / 6'1"	1'10" / 3'4"	1'5" / 3'4"	3'6" / 5'3"	2'10" / 5'3"	2'2" / 5'3"	NA / NA
3	3'1" / 4'2"	2'8" / 3'8"	2'3" / 3'8"	2'0" / 3'8"	3'1" / 7'4"	2'2" / 4'0"	1'8" / 4'0"	4'2" / 6'3"	3'5" / 6'3"	2'8" / 6'3"	NA / NA
3½	3'8" / 4'10"	3'1" / 4'3"	2'7" / 4'3"	2'4" / 4'3"	3'7" / 8'7"	2'6" / 4'8"	1'11" / 4'8"	4'10" / 7'4"	4'0" / 7'4"	3'1" / 7'4"	NA / NA
4	4'2" / 5'6"	3'7" / 4'11"	2'11" / 4'11"	2'8" / 4'11"	4'2" / 9'9"	2'11" / 5'4"	2'3" / 5'4"	5'6" / 8'5"	4'6" / 8'5"	3'6" / 8'5"	NA / NA
4½	4'8" / 6'3"	4'0" / 5'6"	3'4" / 5'6"	3'0" / 5'6"	4'8" / 11'0"	3'3" / 6'0"	2'6" / 6'0"	6'3" / 9'5"	5'1" / 9'5"	3'11" / 9'5"	NA / NA
5	5'2" / 6'11"	4'5" / 6'1"	3'8" / 6'1"	3'4" / 6'1"	5'2" / 12'3"	3'7" / 6'8"	2'9" / 6'8"	6'11" / 10'6"	5'8" / 10'6"	4'5" / 10'6"	NA / NA
5½	5'8" / 7'7"	4'11" / 6'9"	4'1" / 6'9"	3'8" / 6'9"	5'8" / 13'5"	4'0" / 7'4"	3'1" / 7'4"	7'7" / 11'6"	6'3" / 11'6"	4'10" / 11'6"	NA / NA
6	6'3" / 8'4"	5'4" / 7'4"	4'5" / 7'4"	4'0" / 7'4"	6'2" / 14'8"	4'4" / 8'0"	3'4" / 8'0"	8'4" / 12'7"	6'10" / 12'7"	5'3" / 12'7"	NA / NA

6½	6'9" 9'0"	5'9" 7'11"	4'9" 7'11"	4'4" 7'11"	6'9" 15'11"	4'8" 8'8"	3'7" 8'8"	9'0" 13'7"	7'4" 13'7"	5'8" 13'7"	NA NA
7	7'3" 9'8"	6'3" 8'7"	5'2" 8'7"	4'7" 8'7"	7'3" 17'1"	5'1" 9'4"	3'11" 9'4"	9'8" 14'8"	7'11" 14'8"	6'2" 14'8"	NA NA
8	8'4" 11'1"	7'1" 9'9"	5'11" 9'9"	5'3" 9'9"	8'3" 19'7"	5'9" 10'8"	4'5" 10'8"	11'1" 16'9"	9'1" 16'9"	7'0" 16'9"	NA NA
9	9'4" 12'6"	8'0" 11'0"	6'8" 11'0"	5'11" 11'0"	9'4" 22'0"	6'6" 12'0"	5'0" 12'0"	12'6" 18'10"	10'2" 18'10"	7'11" 18'10"	NA NA
10	10'4" 13'10"	8'11" 12'3"	7'4" 12'3"	6'7" 12'3"	10'4" 24'5"	7'3" 13'4"	5'7" 13'4"	13'10" 20'11"	11'4" 20'11"	8'9" 20'11"	NA NA
12	12'5" 16'7"	10'8" 14'8"	8'10" 14'8"	7'11" 14'8"	12'5" 29'4"	8'8" 16'0"	6'8" 16'0"	16'7" 25'2"	13'7" 25'2"	10'6" 25'2"	NA NA
14	14'6" 19'5"	12'6" 17'1"	10'4" 17'1"	9'3" 17'1"	14'6" 34'3"	10'1" 18'8"	7'9" 18'8"	19'5" 29'4"	15'10" 29'4"	12'3" 29'4"	NA NA
16	16'7" 22'2"	14'3" 19'7"	11'9" 19'7"	10'7" 19'7"	16'6" 39'1"	11'6" 21'4"	8'11" 21'4"	22'2" 33'6"	18'2" 33'6"	14'0" 33'6"	NA NA
18	18'8" 24'11"	16'0" 22'0"	13'3" 22'0"	11'11" 22'0"	18'7" 44'0"	13'0" 24'0"	10'0" 24'0"	24'11" 37'9"	20'5" 37'9"	15'9" 37'9"	NA NA
20	20'9" 27'8"	17'10" 24'5"	14'9" 24'5"	13'2" 24'5"	20'8" 48'11"	14'5" 26'8"	11'1" 26'8"	27'8" 41'11"	22'8" 41'11"	17'6" 41'11"	NA NA
25	25'11" 34'7"	22'3" 30'7"	18'5" 30'7"	16'6" 30'7"	25'10" 61'1"	18'0" 33'4"	13'11" 33'4"	34'7" 52'5"	28'4" 52'5"	21'11" 52'5"	NA NA
50	51'10" 69'3"	44'6" 61'1"	36'10" 61'1"	33'0" 61'1"	51'8" 122'2"	36'1" 66'8"	27'10" 66'8"	69'3" 104'9"	56'8" 104'9"	43'10" 104'9"	NA NA

SETUPS (Approximate Distance) — 25mm FIELD OF VIEW

	Full Aperture	Academy 1.33:1	Academy 1.66:1	Academy 1.85:1	Anamorphic 2.40:1	Super 35 1.85:1	Super 35 2.40:1	VistaVision	VistaVision 1.85:1	VistaVision 2.40:1	65mm
Ext Close Up	1' 0"	1' 2"	1' 5"	1' 7"	1' 0"	1' 5"	1' 10"	0' 9"	0' 11"	1' 2"	0' 10"
Close Up	1' 7"	1' 10"	2' 2"	2' 5"	1' 7"	2' 3"	2' 11"	1' 2"	1' 5"	1' 10"	1' 3"
Medium Shot	2' 11"	3' 5"	4' 1"	4' 7"	2' 11"	4' 2"	5' 5"	2' 2"	2' 8"	3' 5"	2' 4"
Full Figure	8' 0"	9' 4"	11' 4"	12' 7"	8' 1"	11' 7"	15' 0"	6' 0"	7' 4"	9' 6"	6' 6"
Angle of View	V 40.9° H 52.9°	V 34.0° H 45.5°	V 28.3° H 45.5°	V 25.5° H 45.5°	V 39.2° H 80.9°	V 29.1° H 51.3°	V 22.6° H 53.1°	V 53.4° H 74.1°	V 44.4° H 74.1°	V 35.0° H 74.1°	V 49.4° H 92.9°
2	1' 6" / 2' 0"	1' 3" / 1' 9"	1' 1" / 1' 9"	0' 11" / 1' 9"	1' 6" / 3' 6"	1' 1" / 1' 11"	0' 10" / 1' 11"	2' 0" / 3' 0"	1' 8" / 3' 0"	1' 3" / 3' 0"	1' 10" / 4' 3"
2½	1' 10" / 2' 6"	1' 7" / 2' 2"	1' 4" / 2' 2"	1' 2" / 2' 2"	1' 10" / 4' 5"	1' 4" / 2' 5"	1' 0" / 2' 5"	2' 6" / 3' 9"	2' 0" / 3' 9"	1' 7" / 3' 9"	2' 4" / 5' 3"
3	2' 3" / 3' 0"	1' 11" / 2' 8"	1' 7" / 2' 8"	1' 5" / 2' 8"	2' 3" / 5' 3"	1' 7" / 2' 11"	1' 2" / 2' 11"	3' 0" / 4' 6"	2' 5" / 4' 6"	1' 11" / 4' 6"	2' 9" / 6' 4"
3½	2' 7" / 3' 6"	2' 3" / 3' 1"	1' 10" / 3' 1"	1' 8" / 3' 1"	2' 7" / 6' 2"	1' 10" / 3' 4"	1' 5" / 3' 4"	3' 6" / 5' 3"	2' 10" / 5' 3"	2' 2" / 5' 3"	3' 3" / 7' 4"
4	3' 0" / 4' 0"	2' 7" / 3' 6"	2' 1" / 3' 6"	1' 11" / 3' 6"	3' 0" / 7' 0"	2' 1" / 3' 10"	1' 7" / 3' 10"	4' 0" / 6' 0"	3' 3" / 6' 0"	2' 6" / 6' 0"	3' 8" / 8' 5"
4½	3' 4" / 4' 6"	2' 11" / 4' 0"	2' 5" / 4' 0"	2' 2" / 4' 0"	3' 4" / 7' 11"	2' 4" / 4' 4"	1' 10" / 4' 4"	4' 6" / 6' 9"	3' 8" / 6' 9"	2' 10" / 6' 9"	4' 2" / 9' 6"
5	3' 9" / 5' 0"	3' 2" / 4' 5"	2' 8" / 4' 5"	2' 5" / 4' 5"	3' 9" / 8' 10"	2' 7" / 4' 10"	2' 0" / 4' 10"	5' 0" / 7' 7"	4' 1" / 7' 7"	3' 2" / 7' 7"	4' 7" / 10' 6"
5½	4' 1" / 5' 6"	3' 6" / 4' 10"	2' 11" / 4' 10"	2' 7" / 4' 10"	4' 1" / 9' 8"	2' 10" / 5' 3"	2' 2" / 5' 3"	5' 6" / 8' 4"	4' 6" / 8' 4"	3' 6" / 8' 4"	5' 1" / 11' 7"
6	4' 6" / 6' 0"	3' 10" / 5' 3"	3' 2" / 5' 3"	2' 10" / 5' 3"	4' 6" / 10' 7"	3' 1" / 5' 9"	2' 5" / 5' 9"	6' 0" / 9' 1"	4' 11" / 9' 1"	3' 9" / 9' 1"	5' 6" / 12' 8"

6½	4'10" / 6'6"	4'2" / 5'9"	3'5" / 5'9"	3'1" / 5'9"	4'10" / 11'5"	3'4" / 6'3"	2'7" / 6'3"	6'6" / 9'10"	5'4" / 9'10"	4'1" / 9'10"	6'0" / 13'8"
7	5'3" / 7'0"	4'6" / 6'2"	3'9" / 6'2"	3'4" / 6'2"	5'2" / 12'4"	3'8" / 6'9"	2'10" / 6'9"	7'0" / 10'7"	5'9" / 10'7"	4'5" / 10'7"	6'5" / 14'9"
8	6'0" / 8'0"	5'2" / 7'0"	4'3" / 7'0"	3'10" / 7'0"	5'11" / 14'1"	4'2" / 7'8"	3'2" / 7'8"	8'0" / 12'1"	6'6" / 12'1"	5'1" / 12'1"	7'4" / 16'10"
9	6'9" / 9'0"	5'9" / 7'11"	4'9" / 7'11"	4'3" / 7'11"	6'8" / 15'10"	4'8" / 8'8"	3'7" / 8'8"	9'0" / 13'7"	7'4" / 13'7"	5'8" / 13'7"	8'3" / 18'11"
10	7'6" / 10'0"	6'5" / 8'10"	5'4" / 8'10"	4'9" / 8'10"	7'5" / 17'7"	5'2" / 9'7"	4'0" / 9'7"	10'0" / 15'1"	8'2" / 15'1"	6'4" / 15'1"	9'2" / 21'1"
12	9'0" / 12'0"	7'8" / 10'7"	6'4" / 10'7"	5'8" / 10'7"	8'11" / 21'1"	6'3" / 11'6"	4'10" / 11'6"	12'0" / 18'1"	9'9" / 18'1"	7'7" / 18'1"	11'1" / 25'3"
14	10'5" / 13'11"	9'0" / 12'4"	7'5" / 12'4"	6'8" / 12'4"	10'5" / 24'8"	7'3" / 13'5"	5'7" / 13'5"	13'11" / 21'1"	11'5" / 21'1"	8'10" / 21'1"	12'11" / 29'6"
16	11'11" / 15'11"	10'3" / 14'1"	8'6" / 14'1"	7'7" / 14'1"	11'11" / 28'2"	8'4" / 15'4"	6'5" / 15'4"	15'11" / 24'2"	13'1" / 24'2"	10'1" / 24'2"	14'9" / 33'8"
18	13'5" / 17'11"	11'6" / 15'10"	9'7" / 15'10"	8'7" / 15'10"	13'5" / 31'8"	9'4" / 17'3"	7'2" / 17'3"	17'11" / 27'2"	14'8" / 27'2"	11'4" / 27'2"	16'7" / 37'11"
20	14'11" / 19'11"	12'10" / 17'7"	10'7" / 17'7"	9'6" / 17'7"	14'10" / 35'2"	10'5" / 19'2"	8'0" / 19'2"	19'11" / 30'2"	16'4" / 30'2"	12'7" / 30'2"	18'5" / 42'1"
25	18'8" / 24'11"	16'0" / 22'0"	13'3" / 22'0"	11'11" / 22'0"	18'7" / 44'0"	13'0" / 24'0"	10'0" / 24'0"	24'11" / 37'9"	20'5" / 37'9"	15'9" / 37'9"	23'0" / 52'8"
50	37'4" / 49'10"	32'1" / 44'0"	26'6" / 44'0"	23'9" / 44'0"	37'2" / 88'0"	26'0" / 48'0"	20'0" / 48'0"	49'10" / 75'5"	40'10" / 75'5"	31'7" / 75'5"	46'0" / 105'3"

SETUPS (Approximate Distance)

35mm FIELD OF VIEW

	Full Aperture V 29.9° H 39.2°	Academy 1.33:1 V 24.6° H 33.3°	Academy 1.66:1 V 20.4° H 33.3°	Academy 1.85:1 V 18.4° H 33.3°	Anamorphic 2.40:1 V 28.5° H 62.7°	Super 35 1.85:1 V 21.0° H 37.9°	Super 35 2.40:1 V 16.3° H 37.9°	VistaVision V 39.6° H 56.6°	VistaVision 1.85:1 V 32.5° H 56.6°	VistaVision 2.40:1 V 25.4° H 56.6°	65mm V 36.4° H 73.9°
Ext Close Up	1'5"	1'8"	2'0"	2'2"	1'5"	2'0"	2'7"	1'1"	1'3"	1'8"	1'2"
Close Up	2'2"	2'7"	3'1"	3'5"	2'2"	3'2"	4'1"	1'8"	2'0"	2'7"	1'9"
Medium Shot	4'1"	4'9"	5'9"	6'5"	4'1"	5'10"	7'7"	3'1"	3'9"	4'10"	3'4"
Full Figure	11'3"	13'1"	15'10"	17'8"	11'4"	16'2"	21'0"	8'5"	10'4"	13'4"	9'2"
Angle of View											
2	1'1" / 1'5"	0'11" / 1'3"	0'9" / 1'3"	0'8" / 1'3"	1'1" / 2'6"	0'9" / 1'4"	0'7" / 1'4"	1'5" / 2'2"	1'2" / 2'2"	0'11" / 2'2"	1'4" / 3'0"
2½	1'4" / 1'9"	1'2" / 1'7"	0'11" / 1'7"	0'10" / 1'7"	1'4" / 3'2"	0'11" / 1'9"	0'9" / 1'9"	1'9" / 2'8"	1'5" / 2'8"	1'2" / 2'8"	1'8" / 3'9"
3	1'7" / 2'2"	1'4" / 1'11"	1'2" / 1'11"	1'0" / 1'11"	1'7" / 3'9"	1'1" / 2'1"	0'10" / 2'1"	2'2" / 3'3"	1'9" / 3'3"	1'4" / 3'3"	2'0" / 4'6"
3½	1'10" / 2'6"	1'7" / 2'2"	1'4" / 2'2"	1'2" / 2'2"	1'10" / 4'5"	1'4" / 2'5"	1'0" / 2'5"	2'6" / 3'9"	2'0" / 3'9"	1'7" / 3'9"	2'4" / 5'3"
4	2'2" / 2'10"	1'10" / 2'6"	1'6" / 2'6"	1'4" / 2'6"	2'1" / 5'0"	1'6" / 2'9"	1'2" / 2'9"	2'10" / 4'4"	2'4" / 4'4"	1'10" / 4'4"	2'8" / 6'0"
4½	2'5" / 3'2"	2'1" / 2'10"	1'8" / 2'10"	1'6" / 2'10"	2'5" / 5'8"	1'8" / 3'1"	1'3" / 3'1"	3'2" / 4'10"	2'7" / 4'10"	2'0" / 4'10"	3'0" / 6'9"
5	2'8" / 3'7"	2'3" / 3'2"	1'11" / 3'2"	1'8" / 3'2"	2'8" / 6'3"	1'10" / 3'5"	1'5" / 3'5"	3'7" / 5'5"	2'11" / 5'5"	2'3" / 5'5"	3'3" / 7'6"
5½	2'11" / 3'11"	2'6" / 3'5"	2'1" / 3'5"	1'10" / 3'5"	2'11" / 6'11"	2'0" / 3'9"	1'7" / 3'9"	3'11" / 5'11"	3'2" / 5'11"	2'6" / 5'11"	3'7" / 8'3"
6	3'2" / 4'3"	2'9" / 3'9"	2'3" / 3'9"	2'0" / 3'9"	3'2" / 7'6"	2'3" / 4'1"	1'9" / 4'1"	4'3" / 6'6"	3'6" / 6'6"	2'8" / 6'6"	3'11" / 9'0"

	Col 1	Col 2	Col 3	Col 4	Col 5	Col 6	Col 7	Col 8	Col 9	Col 10	Col 11
6½	3'6" / 4'8"	3'0" / 4'1"	2'6" / 4'1"	2'2" / 4'1"	3'5" / 8'2"	2'5" / 4'5"	1'10" / 4'5"	4'8" / 7'0"	3'9" / 7'0"	2'11" / 7'0"	4'3" / 9'9"
7	3'9" / 5'0"	3'2" / 4'5"	2'8" / 4'5"	2'5" / 4'5"	3'9" / 8'10"	2'7" / 4'10"	2'0" / 4'10"	5'0" / 7'7"	4'1" / 7'7"	3'2" / 7'7"	4'7" / 10'6"
8	4'3" / 5'8"	3'8" / 5'0"	3'0" / 5'0"	2'9" / 5'0"	4'3" / 10'1"	3'0" / 5'6"	2'3" / 5'6"	5'8" / 8'7"	4'8" / 8'7"	3'7" / 8'7"	5'3" / 12'0"
9	4'10" / 6'5"	4'1" / 5'8"	3'5" / 5'8"	3'1" / 5'8"	4'9" / 11'4"	3'4" / 6'2"	2'7" / 6'2"	6'5" / 9'8"	5'3" / 9'8"	4'1" / 9'8"	5'11" / 13'6"
10	5'4" / 7'1"	4'7" / 6'3"	3'9" / 6'3"	3'5" / 6'3"	5'4" / 12'7"	3'9" / 6'10"	2'10" / 6'10"	7'1" / 10'9"	5'10" / 10'9"	4'6" / 10'9"	6'7" / 15'0"
12	6'5" / 8'7"	5'6" / 7'6"	4'7" / 7'6"	4'1" / 7'6"	6'4" / 15'1"	4'5" / 8'3"	3'5" / 8'3"	8'7" / 12'11"	7'0" / 12'11"	5'5" / 12'11"	7'11" / 18'1"
14	7'6" / 10'0"	6'5" / 8'10"	5'4" / 8'10"	4'9" / 8'10"	7'5" / 17'7"	5'2" / 9'7"	4'0" / 9'7"	10'0" / 15'1"	8'2" / 15'1"	6'4" / 15'1"	9'2" / 21'1"
16	8'6" / 11'5"	7'4" / 10'1"	6'1" / 10'1"	5'5" / 10'1"	8'6" / 20'1"	5'11" / 11'0"	4'7" / 11'0"	11'5" / 17'3"	9'4" / 17'3"	7'3" / 17'3"	10'6" / 24'1"
18	9'7" / 12'10"	8'3" / 11'4"	6'10" / 11'4"	6'1" / 11'4"	9'7" / 22'7"	6'8" / 12'4"	5'2" / 12'4"	12'10" / 19'5"	10'6" / 19'5"	8'1" / 19'5"	11'10" / 27'1"
20	10'8" / 14'3"	9'2" / 12'7"	7'7" / 12'7"	6'10" / 12'7"	10'7" / 25'2"	7'5" / 13'9"	5'9" / 13'9"	14'3" / 21'7"	11'8" / 21'7"	9'0" / 21'7"	13'2" / 30'1"
25	13'4" / 17'10"	11'5" / 15'9"	9'6" / 15'9"	8'6" / 15'9"	13'3" / 31'5"	9'3" / 17'2"	7'2" / 17'2"	17'10" / 26'11"	14'7" / 26'11"	11'3" / 26'11"	16'5" / 37'7"
50	26'8" / 35'7"	22'11" / 31'5"	18'11" / 31'5"	17'0" / 31'5"	26'7" / 62'10"	18'7" / 34'3"	14'4" / 34'3"	35'7" / 53'11"	29'2" / 53'11"	22'6" / 53'11"	32'10" / 75'2"

SETUPS (Approximate Distance) — 50mm FIELD OF VIEW

Setup	Full Aperture	Academy 1.33:1	Academy 1.66:1	Academy 1.85:1	Anamorphic 2.40:1	Super 35 1.85:1	Super 35 2.40:1	VistaVision	VistaVision 1.85:1	VistaVision 2.40:1	65mm
Ext Close Up	2' 0"	2' 4"	2' 10"	3' 2"	2' 0"	2' 11"	3' 9"	1' 6"	1' 10"	2' 5"	1' 8"
Close Up	3' 1"	3' 8"	4' 5"	4' 11"	3' 2"	4' 6"	5' 10"	2' 4"	2' 10"	3' 8"	2' 6"
Medium Shot	5' 10"	6' 9"	8' 2"	9' 1"	5' 10"	8' 4"	10' 0"	4' 4"	5' 4"	6' 10"	4' 8"
Full Figure	16' 1"	18' 9"	22' 8"	25' 3"	16' 2"	23' 1"	30' 0"	12' 0"	14' 9"	19' 0"	13' 0"
Angle of View	V 21.1° H 28.0°	V 17.4° H 23.7°	V 14.4° H 23.7°	V 12.9° H 23.7°	V 20.2° H 46.2°	V 14.8° H 27.0°	V 11.4° H 27.0°	V 28.3° H 41.3°	V 23.1° H 41.3°	V 17.9° H 41.3°	V 24.9° H 51.8°
2	0' 9" / 1' 0"	0' 8" / 0' 11"	0' 6" / 0' 11"	0' 6" / 0' 11"	0' 9" / 1' 9"	0' 6" / 1' 0"	0' 5" / 1' 0"	1' 0" / 1' 6"	0' 10" / 1' 6"	0' 8" / 1' 6"	0' 11" / 2' 1"
2½	0' 11" / 1' 3"	0' 10" / 1' 1"	0' 8" / 1' 1"	0' 7" / 1' 1"	0' 11" / 2' 2"	0' 8" / 1' 2"	0' 6" / 1' 2"	1' 3" / 1' 11"	1' 0" / 1' 11"	0' 9" / 1' 11"	1' 2" / 2' 8"
3	1' 1" / 1' 6"	1' 0" / 1' 4"	0' 10" / 1' 4"	0' 9" / 1' 4"	1' 1" / 2' 8"	0' 9" / 1' 5"	0' 7" / 1' 5"	1' 6" / 2' 3"	1' 3" / 2' 3"	0' 11" / 2' 3"	1' 5" / 3' 2"
3½	1' 4" / 1' 9"	1' 2" / 1' 6"	0' 11" / 1' 6"	0' 10" / 1' 6"	1' 4" / 3' 1"	0' 11" / 1' 8"	0' 8" / 1' 8"	1' 9" / 2' 8"	1' 5" / 2' 8"	1' 1" / 2' 8"	1' 7" / 3' 8"
4	1' 6" / 2' 0"	1' 3" / 1' 9"	1' 1" / 1' 9"	0' 11" / 1' 9"	1' 6" / 3' 6"	1' 0" / 1' 11"	0' 10" / 1' 11"	2' 0" / 3' 0"	1' 8" / 3' 0"	1' 3" / 3' 0"	1' 10" / 4' 3"
4½	1' 8" / 2' 3"	1' 5" / 2' 0"	1' 2" / 2' 0"	1' 1" / 2' 0"	1' 8" / 4' 0"	1' 2" / 2' 2"	0' 11" / 2' 2"	2' 3" / 3' 5"	1' 10" / 3' 5"	1' 5" / 3' 5"	2' 1" / 4' 9"
5	1' 10" / 2' 6"	1' 7" / 2' 2"	1' 4" / 2' 2"	1' 2" / 2' 2"	1' 10" / 4' 5"	1' 4" / 2' 5"	1' 0" / 2' 5"	2' 6" / 3' 9"	2' 0" / 3' 9"	1' 7" / 3' 9"	2' 4" / 5' 3"
5½	2' 1" / 2' 9"	1' 9" / 2' 5"	1' 6" / 2' 5"	1' 4" / 2' 5"	2' 1" / 4' 10"	1' 5" / 2' 8"	1' 1" / 2' 8"	2' 9" / 4' 2"	2' 3" / 4' 2"	1' 9" / 4' 2"	2' 6" / 5' 9"
6	2' 3" / 3' 0"	1' 11" / 2' 8"	1' 7" / 2' 8"	1' 5" / 2' 8"	2' 3" / 5' 3"	1' 7" / 2' 11"	1' 2" / 2' 11"	3' 0" / 4' 6"	2' 5" / 4' 6"	1' 11" / 4' 6"	2' 9" / 6' 4"

6½	2'5" 3'3"	2'1" 2'10"	1'9" 2'10"	1'7" 2'10"	2'5" 5'9"	1'8" 3'1"	1'4" 3'1"	3'3" 4'11"	2'8" 4'11"	2'1" 4'11"	3'0" 6'10"
7	2'7" 3'6"	2'3" 3'1"	1'10" 3'1"	1'8" 3'1"	2'7" 6'2"	1'10" 3'4"	1'5" 3'4"	3'6" 5'3"	2'10" 5'3"	2'2" 5'3"	3'3" 7'4"
8	3'0" 4'0"	2'7" 3'6"	2'1" 3'6"	1'11" 3'6"	3'0" 7'0"	2'1" 3'10"	1'7" 3'10"	4'0" 6'0"	3'3" 6'0"	2'6" 6'0"	3'8" 8'5"
9	3'4" 4'6"	2'11" 4'0"	2'5" 4'0"	2'2" 4'0"	3'4" 7'11"	2'4" 4'4"	1'10" 4'4"	4'6" 6'9"	3'8" 6'9"	2'10" 6'9"	4'2" 9'6"
10	3'9" 5'0"	3'2" 4'5"	2'8" 4'5"	2'5" 4'5"	3'9" 8'10"	2'7" 4'10"	2'0" 4'10"	5'0" 7'7"	4'1" 7'7"	3'2" 7'7"	4'7" 10'6"
12	4'6" 6'0"	3'10" 5'3"	3'2" 5'3"	2'10" 5'3"	4'6" 10'7"	3'1" 5'9"	2'5" 5'9"	6'0" 9'1"	4'11" 9'1"	3'9" 9'1"	5'6" 12'8"
14	5'3" 7'0"	4'6" 6'2"	3'9" 6'2"	3'4" 6'2"	5'2" 12'4"	3'8" 6'9"	2'10" 6'9"	7'0" 10'7"	5'9" 10'7"	4'5" 10'7"	6'5" 14'9"
16	6'0" 8'0"	5'2" 7'0"	4'3" 7'0"	3'10" 7'0"	5'11" 14'1"	4'2" 7'8"	3'2" 7'8"	8'0" 12'1"	6'6" 12'1"	5'1" 12'1"	7'4" 16'10"
18	6'9" 9'0"	5'9" 7'11"	4'9" 7'11"	4'3" 7'11"	6'8" 15'10"	4'8" 8'8"	3'7" 8'8"	9'0" 13'7"	7'4" 13'7"	5'8" 13'7"	8'3" 18'11"
20	7'6" 10'0"	6'5" 8'10"	5'4" 8'10"	4'9" 8'10"	7'5" 17'7"	5'2" 9'7"	4'0" 9'7"	10'0" 15'1"	8'2" 15'1"	6'4" 15'1"	9'2" 21'1"
25	9'4" 12'6"	8'0" 11'0"	6'8" 11'0"	5'11" 11'0"	9'4" 22'0"	6'6" 12'0"	5'0" 12'0"	12'6" 18'10"	10'2" 18'10"	7'11" 18'10"	11'6" 26'4"
50	18'8" 24'11"	16'0" 22'0"	13'3" 22'0"	11'11" 22'0"	18'7" 44'0"	13'0" 24'0"	10'0" 24'0"	24'11" 37'9"	20'5" 37'9"	15'9" 37'9"	23'0" 52'8"

85mm FIELD OF VIEW

SETUPS (Approximate Distance)

	Full Aperture	Academy 1.33:1	Academy 1.66:1	Academy 1.85:1	Anamorphic 2.40:1	Super 35 1.85:1	Super 35 2.40:1	VistaVision	VistaVision 1.85:1	VistaVision 2.40:1	65mm
Ext Close Up	3' 5"	4' 0"	4' 10"	5' 4"	3' 5"	4' 11"	6' 4"	2' 7"	3' 2"	4' 0"	2' 9"
Close Up	5' 4"	6' 2"	7' 6"	8' 4"	5' 4"	7' 8"	9' 11"	4' 0"	4' 10"	6' 3"	4' 4"
Medium Shot	9' 10"	11' 6"	13' 11"	15' 6"	9' 11"	14' 2"	18' 5"	7' 5"	9' 0"	11' 8"	8' 0"
Full Figure	27' 4"	31' 10"	38' 6"	42' 11"	27' 5"	39' 4"	51' 0"	20' 6"	25' 0"	32' 4"	22' 2"

Angle of View	Full Aperture V 12.5° H 16.7°	Academy 1.33:1 V 10.3° H 14.1°	Academy 1.66:1 V 8.5° H 14.1°	Academy 1.85:1 V 7.6° H 14.1°	Anamorphic 2.40:1 V 11.9° H 28.1°	Super 35 1.85:1 V 8.7° H 16.1°	Super 35 2.40:1 V 6.7° H 16.1°	VistaVision V 16.8° H 25.0°	VistaVision 1.85:1 V 13.7° H 25.0°	VistaVision 2.40:1 V 10.6° H 25.0°	65mm
2	0' 5" / 0' 7"	0' 5" / 0' 6"	0' 4" / 0' 6"	0' 3" / 0' 6"	0' 5" / 1' 0"	0' 4" / 0' 7"	0' 3" / 0' 7"	0' 7" / 0' 11"	0' 6" / 0' 11"	0' 4" / 0' 11"	NA NA
2½	0' 7" / 0' 9"	0' 6" / 0' 8"	0' 5" / 0' 8"	0' 4" / 0' 8"	0' 7" / 1' 4"	0' 5" / 0' 8"	0' 4" / 0' 8"	0' 9" / 1' 1"	0' 7" / 1' 1"	0' 6" / 1' 1"	NA NA
3	0' 8" / 0' 11"	0' 7" / 0' 9"	0' 6" / 0' 9"	0' 5" / 0' 9"	0' 8" / 1' 7"	0' 5" / 0' 10"	0' 4" / 0' 10"	0' 11" / 1' 4"	0' 9" / 1' 4"	0' 7" / 1' 4"	NA NA
3½	0' 9" / 1' 0"	0' 8" / 0' 11"	0' 7" / 0' 11"	0' 6" / 0' 11"	0' 9" / 1' 10"	0' 6" / 1' 0"	0' 5" / 1' 0"	1' 0" / 1' 7"	0' 10" / 1' 7"	0' 8" / 1' 7"	NA NA
4	0' 11" / 1' 2"	0' 9" / 1' 0"	0' 7" / 1' 0"	0' 7" / 1' 0"	0' 10" / 2' 1"	0' 7" / 1' 2"	0' 6" / 1' 2"	1' 2" / 1' 9"	1' 0" / 1' 9"	0' 9" / 1' 9"	NA NA
4½	1' 0" / 1' 4"	0' 10" / 1' 2"	0' 8" / 1' 2"	0' 8" / 1' 2"	1' 0" / 2' 4"	0' 8" / 1' 3"	0' 6" / 1' 3"	1' 4" / 2' 0"	1' 1" / 2' 0"	1' 0" / 2' 0"	NA NA
5	1' 1" / 1' 6"	0' 11" / 1' 4"	0' 9" / 1' 4"	0' 8" / 1' 4"	1' 1" / 2' 7"	0' 9" / 1' 5"	0' 7" / 1' 5"	1' 6" / 2' 3"	1' 2" / 2' 3"	0' 11" / 2' 3"	NA NA
5½	1' 2" / 1' 7"	1' 0" / 1' 5"	0' 10" / 1' 5"	0' 9" / 1' 5"	1' 2" / 2' 10"	0' 10" / 1' 7"	0' 8" / 1' 7"	1' 7" / 2' 5"	1' 4" / 2' 5"	1' 0" / 2' 5"	NA NA
6	1' 4" / 1' 9"	1' 2" / 1' 7"	0' 11" / 1' 7"	0' 10" / 1' 7"	1' 4" / 3' 1"	0' 11" / 1' 8"	0' 8" / 1' 8"	1' 9" / 2' 8"	1' 5" / 2' 8"	1' 1" / 2' 8"	NA NA

6½	1'5" 1'11"	1'3" 1'8"	1'0" 1'8"	0'11" 1'8"	1'5" 3'4"	1'0" 1'10"	0'9" 1'10"	1'11" 2'11"	1'7" 2'11"	1'2" 2'11"	NA NA
7	1'6" 2'1"	1'4" 1'10"	1'1" 1'10"	1'0" 1'10"	1'6" 3'7"	1'1" 2'0"	0'10" 2'0"	2'1" 3'1"	1'8" 3'1"	1'4" 3'1"	NA NA
8	1'9" 2'4"	1'6" 2'1"	1'3" 2'1"	1'1" 2'1"	1'9" 4'2"	1'3" 2'3"	0'11" 2'3"	2'4" 3'7"	1'11" 3'7"	1'6" 3'7"	NA NA
9	2'0" 2'8"	1'8" 2'4"	1'5" 2'4"	1'3" 2'4"	2'0" 4'8"	1'4" 2'6"	1'1" 2'6"	2'8" 4'0"	2'2" 4'0"	1'8" 4'0"	NA NA
10	2'2" 2'11"	1'11" 2'7"	1'7" 2'7"	1'5" 2'7"	2'2" 5'2"	1'6" 2'10"	1'2" 2'10"	2'11" 4'5"	2'5" 4'5"	1'10" 4'5"	NA NA
12	2'8" 3'6"	2'3" 3'1"	1'10" 3'1"	1'8" 3'1"	2'7" 6'3"	1'10" 3'5"	1'5" 3'5"	3'6" 5'4"	2'11" 5'4"	2'3" 5'4"	NA NA
14	3'1" 4'1"	2'8" 3'7"	2'2" 3'7"	1'11" 3'7"	3'1" 7'3"	2'2" 3'11"	1'8" 3'11"	4'1" 6'3"	3'4" 6'3"	2'7" 6'3"	NA NA
16	3'6" 4'8"	3'0" 4'2"	2'6" 4'2"	2'3" 4'2"	3'6" 8'3"	2'5" 4'6"	1'11" 4'6"	4'8" 7'1"	3'10" 7'1"	3'0" 7'1"	NA NA
18	3'11" 5'3"	3'5" 4'8"	2'10" 4'8"	2'6" 4'8"	3'11" 9'4"	2'9" 5'1"	2'1" 5'1"	5'3" 8'0"	4'4" 8'0"	3'4" 8'0"	NA NA
20	4'5" 5'10"	3'9" 5'2"	3'1" 5'2"	2'10" 5'2"	4'4" 10'4"	3'1" 5'8"	2'4" 5'8"	5'10" 8'11"	4'10" 8'11"	3'9" 8'11"	NA NA
25	5'6" 7'4"	4'9" 6'6"	3'11" 6'6"	3'6" 6'6"	5'6" 12'11"	3'10" 7'1"	2'11" 7'1"	7'4" 11'1"	6'0" 11'1"	4'8" 11'1"	NA NA
50	11'0" 14'8"	9'5" 12'11"	7'10" 12'11"	7'0" 12'11"	10'11" 25'11"	7'8" 14'1"	5'11" 14'1"	14'8" 22'2"	12'0" 22'2"	9'3" 22'2"	NA NA

SETUPS (Approximate Distance)

100mm FIELD OF VIEW

	Full Aperture	Academy 1.33:1	Academy 1.66:1	Academy 1.85:1	Anamorphic 2.40:1	Super 35 1.85:1	Super 35 2.40:1	VistaVision	VistaVision 1.85:1	VistaVision 2.40:1	65mm
Ext Close Up	4'0"	4'8"	5'8"	6'4"	4'0"	5'9"	7'6"	3'0"	3'8"	4'9"	3'3"
Close Up	6'3"	7'3"	8'10"	9'10"	6'3"	9'0"	11'8"	4'8"	5'9"	7'5"	5'1"
Medium Shot	11'7"	13'6"	16'4"	18'3"	11'8"	16'8"	21'8"	8'8"	10'7"	13'9"	9'5"
Full Figure	32'2"	37'5"	45'3"	50'6"	32'3"	46'3"	59'11"	24'1"	29'5"	38'0"	26'1"
Angle of View	V 10.7° H 14.2°	V 8.7° H 12.0°	V 7.2° H 12.0°	V 6.5° H 12.0°	V 10.2° H 24.1°	V 7.4° H 13.7°	V 5.7° H 13.7°	V 14.3° H 21.4°	V 11.6° H 21.4°	V 9.0° H 21.4°	V 12.6° H 27.3°
2	0'4" / 0'6"	0'4" / 0'5"	0'3" / 0'5"	0'3" / 0'5"	0'4" / 0'11"	0'3" / 0'6"	0'2" / 0'6"	0'6" / 0'9"	0'5" / 0'9"	0'4" / 0'9"	0'6" / 1'1"
2½	0'6" / 0'7"	0'5" / 0'7"	0'4" / 0'7"	0'4" / 0'7"	0'6" / 1'1"	0'4" / 0'7"	0'3" / 0'7"	0'7" / 0'11"	0'6" / 0'11"	0'5" / 0'11"	0'7" / 1'4"
3	0'7" / 0'9"	0'6" / 0'8"	0'5" / 0'8"	0'4" / 0'8"	0'7" / 1'4"	0'5" / 0'9"	0'4" / 0'9"	0'9" / 1'2"	0'7" / 1'2"	0'6" / 1'2"	0'8" / 1'7"
3½	0'8" / 0'10"	0'7" / 0'9"	0'6" / 0'9"	0'5" / 0'9"	0'8" / 1'6"	0'5" / 0'10"	0'4" / 0'10"	0'10" / 1'4"	0'9" / 1'4"	0'7" / 1'4"	0'10" / 1'10"
4	0'9" / 1'0"	0'8" / 0'11"	0'6" / 0'11"	0'6" / 0'11"	0'9" / 1'9"	0'6" / 1'0"	0'5" / 1'0"	1'0" / 1'6"	0'10" / 1'6"	0'8" / 1'6"	0'11" / 2'1"
4½	0'10" / 1'1"	0'9" / 1'0"	0'7" / 1'0"	0'6" / 1'0"	0'10" / 2'0"	0'7" / 1'1"	0'5" / 1'1"	1'1" / 1'8"	0'11" / 1'8"	0'9" / 1'8"	1'0" / 2'4"
5	0'11" / 1'3"	0'10" / 1'1"	0'8" / 1'1"	0'7" / 1'1"	0'11" / 2'2"	0'8" / 1'2"	0'6" / 1'2"	1'3" / 1'11"	1'0" / 1'11"	0'9" / 1'11"	1'2" / 2'8"
5½	1'0" / 1'4"	0'11" / 1'3"	0'9" / 1'3"	0'8" / 1'3"	1'0" / 2'5"	0'9" / 1'4"	0'7" / 1'4"	1'4" / 2'1"	1'1" / 2'1"	0'10" / 2'1"	1'3" / 2'11"
6	1'1" / 1'6"	1'0" / 1'4"	0'10" / 1'4"	0'9" / 1'4"	1'1" / 2'8"	0'9" / 1'5"	0'7" / 1'5"	1'6" / 2'3"	1'3" / 2'3"	0'11" / 2'3"	1'5" / 3'2"

6½	1'3" / 1'7"	1'1" / 1'5"	0'10" / 1'5"	0'9" / 1'5"	1'3" / 2'10"	0'10" / 1'7"	0'8" / 1'7"	1'7" / 2'5"	1'4" / 2'5"	1'0" / 2'5"	1'6" / 3'5"
7	1'4" / 1'9"	1'1" / 1'6"	0'11" / 1'6"	0'10" / 1'6"	1'4" / 3'1"	0'11" / 1'8"	0'8" / 1'8"	1'9" / 2'8"	1'5" / 2'8"	1'1" / 2'8"	1'7" / 3'8"
8	1'6" / 2'0"	1'3" / 1'9"	1'1" / 1'9"	0'11" / 1'9"	1'6" / 3'6"	1'0" / 1'11"	0'10" / 1'11"	2'0" / 3'0"	1'8" / 3'0"	1'3" / 3'0"	1'10" / 4'3"
9	1'8" / 2'3"	1'5" / 2'0"	1'2" / 2'0"	1'1" / 2'0"	1'8" / 4'0"	1'2" / 2'2"	0'11" / 2'2"	2'3" / 3'5"	1'10" / 3'5"	1'5" / 3'5"	2'1" / 4'9"
10	1'10" / 2'6"	1'7" / 2'2"	1'4" / 2'2"	1'2" / 2'2"	1'10" / 4'5"	1'4" / 2'5"	1'0" / 2'5"	2'6" / 3'9"	2'0" / 3'9"	1'7" / 3'9"	2'4" / 5'3"
12	2'3" / 3'0"	1'11" / 2'8"	1'7" / 2'8"	1'5" / 2'8"	2'3" / 5'3"	1'7" / 2'11"	1'2" / 2'11"	3'0" / 4'6"	2'5" / 4'6"	1'11" / 4'6"	2'9" / 6'4"
14	2'7" / 3'6"	2'3" / 3'1"	1'10" / 3'1"	1'8" / 3'1"	2'7" / 6'2"	1'10" / 3'4"	1'5" / 3'4"	3'6" / 5'3"	2'10" / 5'3"	2'2" / 5'3"	3'3" / 7'4"
16	3'0" / 4'0"	2'7" / 3'6"	2'1" / 3'6"	1'11" / 3'6"	3'0" / 7'0"	2'1" / 3'10"	1'7" / 3'10"	4'0" / 6'0"	3'3" / 6'0"	2'6" / 6'0"	3'8" / 8'5"
18	3'4" / 4'6"	2'11" / 4'0"	2'5" / 4'0"	2'2" / 4'0"	3'4" / 7'11"	2'4" / 4'4"	1'10" / 4'4"	4'6" / 6'9"	3'8" / 6'9"	2'10" / 6'9"	4'2" / 9'6"
20	3'9" / 5'0"	3'2" / 4'5"	2'8" / 4'5"	2'5" / 4'5"	3'9" / 8'10"	2'7" / 4'10"	2'0" / 4'10"	5'0" / 7'7"	4'1" / 7'7"	3'2" / 7'7"	4'7" / 10'6"
25	4'8" / 6'3"	4'0" / 5'6"	3'4" / 5'6"	3'0" / 5'6"	4'8" / 11'0"	3'3" / 6'0"	2'6" / 6'0"	6'3" / 9'5"	5'1" / 9'5"	3'11" / 9'5"	5'9" / 13'2"
50	9'4" / 12'6"	8'0" / 11'0"	6'8" / 11'0"	5'11" / 11'0"	9'4" / 22'0"	6'6" / 12'0"	5'0" / 12'0"	12'6" / 18'10"	10'2" / 18'10"	7'11" / 18'10"	11'6" / 26'4"

SETUPS (Approximate Distance)

200mm FIELD OF VIEW

	Full Aperture	Academy 1.33:1	Academy 1.66:1	Academy 1.85:1	Anamorphic 2.40:1	Super 35 1.85:1	Super 35 2.40:1	VistaVision	VistaVision 1.85:1	VistaVision 2.40:1	65mm
Ext Close Up	8'0"	9'4"	11'4"	12'7"	8'1"	11'7"	15'0"	6'0"	7'4"	9'6"	6'6"
Close Up	12'6"	14'7"	17'7"	19'8"	12'7"	18'0"	23'4"	9'4"	11'5"	14'10"	10'2"
Medium Shot	23'3"	27'0"	32'8"	36'5"	23'4"	33'5"	43'4"	17'5"	21'3"	27'6"	18'10"
Full Figure	64'3"	74'10"	90'6"	100'11"	64'6"	92'5"	119'11"	48'2"	58'10"	76'1"	52'2"
Angle of View	V 5.3° H 7.1°	V 4.4° H 6.0°	V 3.6° H 6.0°	V 3.2° H 6.0°	V 5.1° H 12.2°	V 3.7° H 6.9°	V 2.9° H 6.9°	V 7.2° H 10.8°	V 5.8° H 10.8°	V 4.5° H 10.8°	V 6.6° H 15.0°
5	0'6" / 0'7"	0'5" / 0'7"	0'4" / 0'7"	0'4" / 0'7"	0'6" / 1'1"	0'4" / 0'7"	0'3" / 0'7"	0'7" / 0'11"	0'6" / 0'11"	0'5" / 0'11"	0'7" / 1'4"
5½	0'6" / 0'8"	0'5" / 0'7"	0'4" / 0'7"	0'4" / 0'7"	0'6" / 1'3"	0'4" / 0'8"	0'3" / 0'8"	0'8" / 1'0"	0'7" / 1'0"	0'5" / 1'0"	0'8" / 1'5"
6	0'7" / 0'9"	0'6" / 0'8"	0'5" / 0'8"	0'4" / 0'8"	0'7" / 1'4"	0'5" / 0'9"	0'4" / 0'9"	0'9" / 1'2"	0'7" / 1'2"	0'6" / 1'2"	0'8" / 1'7"
6½	0'7" / 0'10"	0'6" / 0'9"	0'5" / 0'9"	0'5" / 0'9"	0'7" / 1'5"	0'5" / 0'9"	0'4" / 0'9"	0'10" / 1'3"	0'8" / 1'3"	0'6" / 1'3"	0'9" / 1'9"
7	0'8" / 0'10"	0'7" / 0'9"	0'6" / 0'9"	0'5" / 0'9"	0'8" / 1'6"	0'5" / 0'10"	0'4" / 0'10"	0'10" / 1'4"	0'9" / 1'4"	0'7" / 1'4"	0'10" / 1'10"
8	0'9" / 1'0"	0'8" / 0'11"	0'6" / 0'11"	0'6" / 0'11"	0'9" / 1'9"	0'6" / 1'0"	0'5" / 1'0"	1'0" / 1'6"	0'9" / 1'6"	0'8" / 1'6"	0'11" / 2'1"
9	0'10" / 1'1"	0'9" / 1'0"	0'7" / 1'0"	0'6" / 1'0"	0'10" / 2'0"	0'7" / 1'1"	0'5" / 1'1"	1'1" / 1'8"	0'11" / 1'8"	0'9" / 1'8"	1'0" / 2'4"
10	0'11" / 1'3"	0'10" / 1'1"	0'8" / 1'1"	0'7" / 1'1"	0'11" / 2'2"	0'8" / 1'2"	0'6" / 1'2"	1'3" / 1'11"	1'0" / 1'11"	0'9" / 1'11"	1'2" / 2'8"
12	1'1" / 1'6"	1'0" / 1'4"	0'10" / 1'4"	0'9" / 1'4"	1'1" / 2'8"	0'9" / 1'5"	0'7" / 1'5"	1'6" / 2'3"	1'3" / 2'3"	0'11" / 2'3"	1'5" / 3'2"

14	1'4"/1'9"	1'1"/1'6"	0'11"/1'6"	0'10"/1'6"	1'4"/3'1"	0'11"/1'8"	0'8"/1'8"	1'9"/2'8"	1'5"/2'8"	1'1"/2'8"	1'7"/3'8"
16	1'6"/2'0"	1'3"/1'9"	1'1"/1'9"	0'11"/1'9"	1'6"/3'6"	1'0"/1'11"	0'10"/1'11"	2'0"/3'0"	1'8"/3'0"	1'3"/3'0"	1'10"/4'3"
18	1'8"/2'3"	1'5"/2'0"	1'2"/2'0"	1'1"/2'0"	1'8"/4'0"	1'2"/2'2"	0'11"/2'2"	2'3"/3'5"	1'10"/3'5"	1'5"/3'5"	2'1"/4'9"
20	1'10"/2'6"	1'7"/2'2"	1'4"/2'2"	1'2"/2'2"	1'10"/4'5"	1'4"/2'5"	1'0"/2'5"	2'6"/3'9"	2'0"/3'9"	1'7"/3'9"	2'4"/5'3"
25	2'4"/3'1"	2'0"/2'9"	1'8"/2'9"	1'6"/2'9"	2'4"/5'6"	1'7"/3'0"	1'3"/3'0"	3'1"/4'9"	2'7"/4'9"	2'0"/4'9"	2'11"/6'7"
50	4'8"/6'3"	4'0"/5'6"	3'4"/5'6"	3'0"/5'6"	4'8"/11'0"	3'3"/6'0"	2'6"/6'0"	6'3"/9'5"	5'1"/9'5"	3'11"/9'5"	5'9"/13'2"
75	7'0"/9'4"	6'0"/8'3"	5'0"/8'3"	4'5"/8'3"	7'0"/16'6"	4'10"/9'0"	3'9"/9'0"	9'4"/14'2"	7'8"/14'2"	5'11"/14'2"	8'8"/19'9"
100	9'4"/12'6"	8'0"/11'0"	6'8"/11'0"	5'11"/11'0"	9'4"/22'0"	6'6"/12'0"	5'0"/12'0"	12'6"/18'10"	10'2"/18'10"	7'11"/18'10"	11'6"/26'4"
125	11'8"/15'7"	10'0"/13'9"	8'3"/13'9"	7'5"/13'9"	11'7"/27'6"	8'1"/15'0"	6'3"/15'0"	15'7"/23'7"	12'9"/23'7"	9'10"/23'7"	14'5"/32'11"
150	14'0"/18'8"	12'0"/16'6"	9'11"/16'6"	8'11"/16'6"	13'11"/33'0"	9'9"/18'0"	7'6"/18'0"	18'8"/28'3"	15'4"/28'3"	11'10"/28'3"	17'3"/39'6"
175	16'4"/21'10"	14'0"/19'3"	11'7"/19'3"	10'5"/19'3"	16'3"/38'6"	11'4"/21'0"	8'9"/21'0"	21'10"/33'0"	17'10"/33'0"	13'10"/33'0"	20'2"/46'1"
200	18'8"/24'11"	16'0"/22'0"	13'3"/22'0"	11'11"/22'0"	18'7"/44'0"	13'0"/24'0"	10'0"/24'0"	24'11"/37'9"	20'5"/37'9"	15'9"/37'9"	23'0"/52'8"

16mm/SUPER 16 — FIELD OF VIEW

SETUPS (Approximate Distance)

LENS SIZE	FORMAT	Ext Cls Up	Close Up	Med Shot	Full Figure	ANGLE OF VIEW (V)	ANGLE OF VIEW (H)	FOCUS 2 ft	FOCUS 2½ ft
5.9mm	16mm					V 63.2°	H 78.6°		
5.9mm	Super16	0'7"	0'11"	1'8"	4'9"	V 56.8°	H 89.8°	2'6" / 3'6"	3'2" / 4'4"
8mm	16mm	0'10"	1'3"	2'4"	6'5"	V 48.8°	H 62.2°	1'10" / 2'7"	2'4" / 3'2"
8mm	Super16	0'11"	1'6"	2'9"	7'6"	V 43.5°	H 72.6°	1'7" / 2'11"	2'0" / 3'8"
10mm	16mm	1'0"	1'7"	2'11"	8'0"	V 39.9°	H 51.5°	1'6" / 2'1"	1'10" / 2'7"
10mm	Super16	1'2"	1'10"	3'5"	9'5"	V 35.4°	H 60.9°	1'3" / 2'4"	1'7" / 2'11"
12mm	16mm	1'2"	1'10"	3'6"	9'7"	V 33.7°	H 43.8°	1'3" / 1'9"	1'7" / 2'2"
12mm	Super16	1'5"	2'2"	4'11"	11'4"	V 29.8°	H 52.2°	0'11" / 2'0"	1'4" / 2'5"
16mm	16mm	1'7"	2'6"	4'8"	12'10"	V 25.6°	H 33.6°	0'11" / 1'3"	1'2" / 1'7"
16mm	Super16	1'11"	2'11"	5'5"	15'1"	V 22.5°	H 40.4°	0'10" / 1'6"	1'0" / 1'10"
25mm	16mm	2'6"	3'11"	7'3"	20'0"	V 16.5°	H 21.9°	0'7" / 0'10"	0'9" / 1'0"
25mm	Super16	2'11"	4'7"	8'6"	23'6"	V 14.5°	H 26.5°	0'6" / 0'11"	0'8" / 1'2"
37.5mm	16mm	3'9"	5'10"	10'10"	30'0"	V 11.1°	H 14.7°	0'5" / 0'7"	0'6" / 0'8"
37.5mm	Super16	4'5"	6'10"	12'9"	35'4"	V 9.7°	H 17.8°	0'4" / 0'8"	0'5" / 0'9"
50mm	16mm	5'0"	7'9"	14'5"	40'0"	V 8.3°	H 11.0°	0'4" / 0'5"	0'4" / 0'6"
50mm	Super16	5'11"	9'2"	17'0"	47'1"	V 7.3°	H 13.4°	0'3" / 0'6"	0'4" / 0'7"
85mm	16mm	8'6"	13'3"	24'7"	68'1"	V 4.9°	H 6.5°	0'2" / 0'2"	0'3" / 0'4"
85mm	Super16	10'0"	15'7"	28'11"	80'0"	V 4.3°	H 7.9°	0'2" / 0'3"	0'4" / 0'5"
100mm	16mm	10'0"	15'7"	28'11"	80'1"	V 4.2°	H 5.5°	0'2" / 0'2"	0'2" / 0'3"
100mm	Super16	11'9"	18'4"	34'0"	94'1"	V 3.7°	H 6.7°	0'2" / 0'3"	0'3" / 0'4"
150mm	16mm	15'0"	23'4"	43'4"	120'1"	V 2.8°	H 3.7°	0'1" / 0'2"	0'1" / 0'2"
150mm	Super16	17'8"	27'5"	51'0"	141'2"	V 2.4°	H 4.5°	0'1" / 0'2"	0'2"
200mm	16mm	20'0"	31'2"	57'10"	160'2"	V 2.1°	H 2.8°	NA	NA
200mm	Super16	23'6"	36'7"	68'0"	188'3"	V 1.8°	H 3.4°	NA	NA
300mm	16mm	30'0"	46'9"	86'9"	240'3"	V 1.4°	H 1.8°	NA	NA
300mm	Super16	35'4"	54'11"	101'11"	282'4"	V 1.2°	H 2.2°	NA	NA
400mm	16mm	40'0"	62'3"	115'8"	320'4"	V 1.0°	H 1.4°	NA	NA
400mm	Super16	47'1"	73'2"	135'11"	376'5"	V 0.9°	H 1.7°	NA	NA

mm																	
3	NA/NA	NA/NA	NA/NA	NA/NA	0'1"/0'2"	0'2"/0'2"	0'2"/0'3"	0'3"/0'4"	0'3"/0'4"	0'5"/0'7"	0'7"/0'10"	0'11"/1'3"	1'5"/1'11"	1'10"/2'7"	2'3"/3'1"	2'10"/3'10"	3'10"/5'3"
																	3'3"/6'0"
3½	NA/NA	NA/NA	NA/NA	0'1"/0'2"	0'1"/0'2"	0'2"/0'2"	0'2"/0'3"	0'3"/0'4"	0'4"/0'5"	0'5"/0'8"	0'8"/0'11"	1'1"/1'5"	1'8"/2'3"	2'2"/3'0"	2'7"/3'7"	3'3"/4'6"	4'5"/6'0"
																	3'9"/7'0"
4	NA/NA	NA/NA	0'1"/0'2"	0'1"/0'2"	0'2"/0'2"	0'2"/0'3"	0'2"/0'3"	0'3"/0'4"	0'4"/0'6"	0'6"/0'9"	0'8"/1'0"	1'2"/1'8"	1'10"/2'7"	2'6"/3'5"	3'0"/4'1"	3'9"/5'2"	5'1"/6'11"
																	4'4"/8'0"
4½	NA/NA	NA/NA	0'1"/0'2"	0'2"/0'2"	0'2"/0'3"	0'2"/0'3"	0'3"/0'4"	0'3"/0'4"	0'4"/0'6"	0'6"/0'11"	0'9"/1'1"	1'4"/1'10"	2'1"/2'11"	2'10"/3'10"	3'4"/4'7"	4'3"/5'9"	5'9"/7'10"
																	4'10"/9'0"
5	NA	0'1"/0'2"	0'2"/0'2"	0'2"/0'3"	0'2"/0'3"	0'3"/0'4"	0'4"/0'6"	0'4"/0'7"	0'5"/0'7"	0'7"/0'11"	0'10"/1'2"	1'6"/2'1"	2'4"/3'2"	3'1"/4'3"	3'9"/5'2"	4'8"/6'5"	6'4"/8'8"
																	5'5"/10'0"
5½	0'1"/0'2"	0'1"/0'2"	0'2"/0'2"	0'2"/0'3"	0'3"/0'4"	0'3"/0'4"	0'4"/0'6"	0'5"/0'7"	0'6"/0'8"	0'8"/1'0"	0'11"/1'3"	1'8"/2'3"	2'7"/3'6"	3'5"/4'8"	4'1"/5'8"	5'2"/7'1"	7'0"/9'7"
																	5'11"/11'0"
6	0'1"/0'2"	0'1"/0'2"	0'2"/0'3"	0'2"/0'3"	0'3"/0'4"	0'4"/0'5"	0'4"/0'7"	0'5"/0'8"	0'6"/0'9"	0'8"/1'0"	1'0"/1'4"	1'10"/2'6"	2'10"/3'10"	3'9"/5'2"	4'6"/6'2"	5'7"/7'8"	7'7"/10'5"
																	6'6"/12'0"
6½	0'1"/0'2"	0'2"/0'2"	0'2"/0'3"	0'2"/0'3"	0'3"/0'4"	0'4"/0'5"	0'4"/0'8"	0'6"/0'8"	0'6"/0'9"	0'9"/1'1"	1'1"/1'5"	2'0"/2'7"	3'1"/4'2"	4'4"/6'0"	4'10"/6'8"	6'1"/8'4"	8'3"/11'4"
																	7'2"/12'11"
7	0'2"/0'2"	0'2"/0'3"	0'2"/0'3"	0'3"/0'3"	0'3"/0'5"	0'4"/0'7"	0'5"/0'9"	0'6"/0'11"	0'7"/0'9"	0'11"/1'5"	1'2"/1'8"	2'1"/2'10"	3'3"/4'6"	4'6"/8'3"	5'3"/7'2"	6'7"/9'0"	8'11"/12'2"
																	7'7"/13'11"

16mm/SUPER 16 — FIELD OF VIEW (continued)

Values are shown for each lens and each format (16mm / Super16) as two stacked dimensions.

FOCUS (feet)	5.9mm 16mm	5.9mm Super16	8mm 16mm	8mm Super16	10mm 16mm	10mm Super16	12mm 16mm	12mm Super16	16mm 16mm	16mm Super16	25mm 16mm	25mm Super16	37.5mm 16mm	37.5mm Super16	50mm 16mm	50mm Super16	85mm 16mm	85mm Super16	100mm 16mm	100mm Super16	150mm 16mm	150mm Super16	200mm 16mm	200mm Super16	300mm 16mm	300mm Super16	400mm 16mm	400mm Super16
8	10'2" / 13'11"	8'8" / 15'11"	7'6" / 10'3"	6'5" / 11'9"	6'0" / 8'3"	5'1" / 9'5"	5'0" / 6'10"	4'3" / 7'10"	3'9" / 5'2"	3'2" / 5'11"	2'5" / 3'3"	2'0" / 3'9"	1'7" / 2'2"	1'4" / 2'6"	1'2" / 1'8"	1'0" / 1'11"	0'8" / 1'0"	0'7" / 1'1"	0'7" / 0'10"	0'6" / 0'11"	0'5" / 0'7"	0'4" / 0'8"	0'4" / 0'5"	0'3" / 0'6"	0'2" / 0'3"	0'2" / 0'4"	0'2" / 0'2"	0'2" / 0'3"
9	11'5" / 15'8"	9'9" / 17'11"	8'5" / 11'7"	7'2" / 13'3"	6'9" / 9'3"	5'9" / 10'7"	5'7" / 7'8"	4'9" / 8'10"	4'3" / 5'9"	3'7" / 6'7"	2'8" / 3'8"	2'4" / 4'3"	1'10" / 2'6"	1'6" / 2'10"	1'4" / 1'10"	1'2" / 2'1"	0'10" / 1'1"	0'8" / 1'3"	0'8" / 0'11"	0'7" / 1'1"	0'5" / 0'7"	0'5" / 0'8"	0'4" / 0'6"	0'4" / 0'7"	0'3" / 0'4"	0'3" / 0'4"	0'2" / 0'3"	0'2" / 0'4"
10	12'8" / 17'5"	10'10" / 19'11"	9'4" / 12'10"	8'0" / 14'8"	7'6" / 10'3"	6'5" / 11'9"	6'3" / 8'7"	5'4" / 9'10"	4'8" / 6'5"	4'0" / 7'4"	3'0" / 4'1"	2'7" / 4'8"	2'0" / 2'9"	1'8" / 3'2"	1'6" / 2'1"	1'3" / 2'4"	0'11" / 1'2"	0'9" / 1'5"	0'9" / 1'0"	0'8" / 1'2"	0'6" / 0'8"	0'5" / 0'9"	0'5" / 0'6"	0'4" / 0'7"	0'3" / 0'4"	0'3" / 0'5"	0'2" / 0'3"	0'2" / 0'4"
12	15'3" / 20'10"	13'0" / 23'11"	11'3" / 15'5"	9'7" / 17'8"	9'0" / 12'4"	7'8" / 14'1"	7'6" / 10'3"	6'5" / 11'9"	5'7" / 7'8"	4'9" / 8'10"	3'7" / 4'11"	3'1" / 5'8"	2'5" / 3'3"	2'0" / 3'9"	1'10" / 2'6"	1'6" / 2'10"	1'1" / 1'5"	1'0" / 1'8"	0'11" / 1'3"	0'9" / 1'5"	0'7" / 0'10"	0'6" / 0'11"	0'6" / 0'8"	0'5" / 0'9"	0'4" / 0'5"	0'3" / 0'6"	0'3" / 0'4"	0'2" / 0'4"
14	17'9" / 24'4"	15'2" / 27'11"	13'1" / 17'11"	11'2" / 20'7"	10'6" / 14'4"	8'11" / 16'6"	8'9" / 12'0"	7'5" / 13'9"	6'7" / 9'0"	5'7" / 10'3"	4'2" / 5'9"	3'7" / 6'7"	2'10" / 3'10"	2'5" / 4'5"	2'1" / 2'10"	1'9" / 3'4"	1'3" / 1'8"	1'1" / 1'11"	1'1" / 1'5"	0'11" / 1'8"	0'8" / 0'11"	0'7" / 1'1"	0'7" / 0'9"	0'6" / 0'10"	0'4" / 0'6"	0'4" / 0'7"	0'3" / 0'4"	0'3" / 0'5"
16	20'4" / 27'10"	17'3" / 31'11"	15'0" / 20'6"	12'9" / 23'6"	12'0" / 16'5"	10'2" / 18'10"	10'0" / 13'8"	8'6" / 15'8"	7'6" / 10'3"	6'5" / 11'9"	4'10" / 6'7"	4'1" / 7'6"	3'2" / 4'5"	2'9" / 5'0"	2'5" / 3'3"	2'0" / 3'9"	1'5" / 1'11"	1'3" / 2'3"	1'2" / 1'8"	1'0" / 1'11"	0'10" / 1'1"	0'8" / 1'3"	0'7" / 0'10"	0'6" / 0'11"	0'5" / 0'7"	0'4" / 0'8"	0'4" / 0'5"	0'3" / 0'6"
18	22'10" / 31'4"	19'5" / 35'11"	16'10" / 23'1"	14'4" / 26'6"	13'6" / 18'6"	11'6" / 21'2"	11'3" / 15'5"	9'7" / 17'8"	8'5" / 11'7"	7'2" / 13'3"	5'5" / 7'5"	4'7" / 8'6"	3'7" / 4'11"	3'1" / 5'8"	2'8" / 3'8"	2'4" / 4'3"	1'7" / 2'2"	1'4" / 2'6"	1'4" / 1'10"	1'2" / 2'1"	0'11" / 1'3"	0'9" / 1'5"	0'8" / 0'11"	0'7" / 1'1"	0'5" / 0'7"	0'5" / 0'8"	0'4" / 0'5"	0'3" / 0'6"

Field-of-view table. Left column = distance (feet); cells give the field width / height (and Super 16mm values in the first column). Focal-length column headings appear on the facing page.

Distance (ft)						
20	25'5" / 34'9" (S16 39'10" / 21'7")	18'9" / 25'8"	15'0" / 20'6"	12'6" / 17'1"	9'4" / 12'10"	6'0" / 8'3"
25	31'9" / 43'6" (S16 49'10" / 27'0")	23'5" / 32'1"	18'9" / 25'8"	15'11" / 21'5"	11'8" / 16'0"	7'6" / 10'3"
50	63'6" / 87'0" (S16 99'8" / 54'0")	46'10" / 64'2"	37'6" / 51'4"	31'3" / 42'9"	23'5" / 32'1"	15'0" / 20'6"
75	95'3" / 130'5" (S16 149'6" / 81'1")	70'3" / 96'2"	56'2" / 77'0"	46'10" / 64'2"	35'1" / 48'1"	22'6" / 30'9"
100	127'0" / 173'11" (S16 199'4" / 108'1")	93'8" / 128'3"	74'11" / 102'7"	62'5" / 85'6"	46'10" / 64'2"	30'0" / 41'1"
125	158'9" / 217'5" (S16 249'2" / 135'1")	117'1" / 160'4"	93'8" / 128'3"	78'1" / 106'11"	58'6" / 80'2"	37'6" / 51'4"
150	190'6" / 260'11" (S16 299'0" / 162'1")	140'6" / 192'5"	112'5" / 153'11"	93'8" / 128'3"	70'3" / 96'2"	44'11" / 61'7"
175	222'3" / 304'4" (S16 348'10" / 189'1")	163'11" / 224'6"	131'1" / 179'7"	109'3" / 149'8"	81'11" / 112'3"	52'5" / 71'10"
200	254'0" / 347'10" (S16 398'8" / 216'1")	187'4" / 256'6"	149'10" / 205'3"	124'11" / 171'0"	93'8" / 128'3"	59'11" / 82'1"

SUPER 8mm/6.5mm CAMERA DEPTH-OF-FIELD, HYPERFOCAL DISTANCE, AND FIELD OF VIEW

CAMERA APERTURE: 0.224 x 0.166 inches
CIRCLE OF CONFUSION=0.0020 inches

Hyperfocal Distance	f/1.4		f/2.0		f/2.8		f/4.0		f/5.6		f/8.0		f/11.0		f/16.0		f/22.0		ANGLE OF VIEW H 47.3° / V 35.9°
	1' 11"		1' 4"		1' 0"		0' 8"		0' 6"		0' 4		0' 3"		0' 2"		0' 1"		
FOCUS	NEAR	FAR	NEAR	FAR	NEAR	FAR	NEAR	FAR	NEAR	FAR	NEAR	FAR	NEAR	FAR	NEAR	FAR	NEAR	FAR	FIELD OF VIEW
2	1' 0"	INF	0' 10"	INF	0' 8"	INF	0' 6"	INF	0' 5"	INF	0' 4"	INF	0' 3"	INF	0' 2"	INF	0' 1"	INF	1' 9" x 1' 3"
4	1' 4"	INF	1' 0"	INF	0' 9"	INF	0' 7"	INF	0' 5"	INF	0' 4"	INF	0' 3"	INF	0' 2"	INF	0' 1"	INF	3' 6" x 2' 7"
6	1' 6"	INF	1' 1"	INF	0' 10"	INF	0' 7"	INF	0' 5"	INF	0' 4"	INF	0' 3"	INF	0' 2"	INF	0' 1"	INF	5' 3" x 3' 11"
8	1' 7"	INF	1' 2"	INF	0' 10"	INF	0' 8"	INF	0' 6"	INF	0' 4"	INF	0' 3"	INF	0' 2"	INF	0' 1"	INF	7' 0" x 5' 2"
10	1' 8"	INF	1' 2"	INF	0' 11"	INF	0' 8"	INF	0' 6"	INF	0' 4"	INF	0' 3"	INF	0' 2"	INF	0' 1"	INF	8' 9" x 6' 6"
12	1' 8"	INF	1' 3"	INF	0' 11"	INF	0' 8"	INF	0' 6"	INF	0' 4"	INF	0' 3"	INF	0' 2"	INF	0' 1"	INF	10' 6" x 7' 9"
16	1' 9"	INF	1' 3"	INF	0' 11"	INF	0' 8"	INF	0' 6"	INF	0' 4"	INF	0' 3"	INF	0' 2"	INF	0' 1"	INF	14' 0" x 10' 4"
25	1' 10"	INF	1' 4"	INF	0' 11"	INF	0' 8"	INF	0' 6"	INF	0' 4"	INF	0' 3"	INF	0' 2"	INF	0' 1"	INF	21' 10" x 16' 2"

SUPER 8mm/13mm CAMERA DEPTH-OF-FIELD, HYPERFOCAL DISTANCE, AND FIELD OF VIEW

CAMERA APERTURE: 0.224 x 0.166 inches · CIRCLE OF CONFUSION=0.0020 inches

FOCUS	f/1.4	f/2.0	f/2.8	f/4.0	f/5.6	f/8.0	f/11.0	f/16.0	f/22.0	FIELD OF VIEW
Hyperfocal Distance	7'10"	5'5"	3'11"	2'9"	1'11"	1'4"	1'0"	0'8"	0'6"	ANGLE OF VIEW H 27.7° / V 18.4°
	NEAR / FAR	NEAR / FAR	NEAR / FAR	NEAR / FAR	NEAR / FAR	NEAR / FAR	NEAR / FAR	NEAR / FAR	NEAR / FAR	
2	1'7" / 2'8"	1'6" / 3'1"	1'4" / 4'0"	1'2" / 7'1"	1'0" / INF	0'10" / INF	0'8" / INF	0'6" / INF	0'5" / INF	0'10" x 0'8"
4	2'8" / 8'1"	2'4" / 14'7"	2'0" / INF	1'8" / INF	1'4" / INF	1'0" / INF	0'10" / INF	0'7" / INF	0'5" / INF	1'9" x 1'3.5"
6	3'5" / 25'5"	2'10" / INF	2'4" / INF	1'11" / INF	1'6" / INF	1'1" / INF	0'10" / INF	0'7" / INF	0'6" / INF	2'7" x 1'11"
8	4'0" / INF	3'3" / INF	2'8" / INF	2'1" / INF	1'7" / INF	1'2" / INF	0'11" / INF	0'8" / INF	0'6" / INF	3'6" x 2'7"
10	4'5" / INF	3'6" / INF	2'10" / INF	2'2" / INF	1'8" / INF	1'2" / INF	0'11" / INF	0'8" / INF	0'6" / INF	4'4" x 3'3"
12	4'9" / INF	3'9" / INF	2'11" / INF	2'3" / INF	1'8" / INF	1'3" / INF	0'11" / INF	0'8" / INF	0'6" / INF	5'3" x 3'11"
16	5'3" / INF	4'1" / INF	3'2" / INF	2'4" / INF	1'9" / INF	1'3" / INF	0'11" / INF	0'8" / INF	0'6" / INF	7'0" x 5'2"
25	5'11" / INF	4'6" / INF	3'5" / INF	2'6" / INF	1'10" / INF	1'4" / INF	0'11" / INF	0'8" / INF	0'6" / INF	10'11" x 8'1"

SUPER 8mm/38mm   CAMERA DEPTH-OF-FIELD, HYPERFOCAL DISTANCE, AND FIELD OF VIEW

CAMERA APERTURE: 0.224 x 0.166 inches

CIRCLE OF CONFUSION=0.0020 inches

	f/1.4	f/2.0	f/2.8	f/4.0	f/5.6	f/8.0	f/11.0	f/16.0	f/22.0	ANGLE OF VIEW H 8.5° / V 6.3°
Hyperfocal Distance	66' 7"	46' 8"	33' 4"	23' 4"	16' 8"	11' 8"	8' 6"	5' 10"	4' 3"	FIELD OF VIEW
FOCUS	NEAR FAR	NEAR FAR	NEAR FAR	NEAR FAR	NEAR FAR	NEAR FAR	NEAR FAR	NEAR FAR	NEAR FAR	
2	1' 11" / 2' 1"	1' 11" / 2' 1"	1' 11" / 2' 1"	1' 10" / 2' 2"	1' 10" / 2' 3"	1' 9" / 2' 5"	1' 8" / 2' 7"	1' 6" / 2' 11"	1' 5" / 3' 7"	0' 4" x 0' 2.6"
4	3' 9" / 4' 3"	3' 8" / 4' 4"	3' 7" / 4' 6"	3' 5" / 4' 10"	3' 3" / 5' 3"	3' 0" / 6' 0"	2' 9" / 7' 4"	2' 5" / 11' 11"	2' 1" / INF	0' 5" x 0' 5.3"
6	5' 6" / 6' 7"	5' 4" / 6' 10"	5' 1" / 7' 3"	4' 10" / 8' 0"	4' 5" / 9' 3"	4' 0" / 12' 1"	3' 7" / 19' 7"	3' 0" / INF	2' 6" / INF	0' 11" x 0' 8"
8	7' 2" / 9' 1"	6' 10" / 9' 8"	6' 6" / 10' 6"	6' 0" / 12' 1"	5' 5" / 15' 2"	4' 9" / 24' 8"	4' 2" / INF	3' 5" / INF	2' 10" / INF	1' 2" x 0' 11"
10	8' 9" / 11' 9"	8' 3" / 12' 8"	7' 9" / 14' 3"	7' 0" / 17' 4"	6' 3" / 24' 7"	5' 5" / 65' 5"	4' 7" / INF	3' 9" / INF	3' 0" / INF	1' 6" x 1' 1"
12	10' 2" / 14' 7"	9' 7" / 16' 1"	8' 10" / 18' 8"	7' 11" / 24' 5"	7' 0" / 41' 10"	5' 11" / INF	5' 0" / INF	3' 11" / INF	3' 2" / INF	1' 9" x 1' 4"
16	12' 11" / 21' 0"	11' 11" / 24' 3"	10' 10" / 30' 7"	9' 6" / 50' 2"	8' 2" / INF	6' 9" / INF	5' 7" / INF	4' 4" / INF	3' 4" / INF	2' 5" x 1' 9"
25	18' 2" / 39' 11"	16' 4" / 53' 7"	14' 4" / 98' 9"	12' 1" / INF	10' 0" / INF	8' 0" / INF	6' 4" / INF	4' 9" / INF	3' 8" / INF	3' 9" x 2' 9"

SUPER 8mm/50mm   CAMERA DEPTH-OF-FIELD, HYPERFOCAL DISTANCE, AND FIELD OF VIEW

CAMERA APERTURE: 0.224 x 0.166 inches   CIRCLE OF CONFUSION=0.0020 inches

Focus		f/1.4	f/2.0	f/2.8	f/4.0	f/5.6	f/8.0	f/11.0	f/16.0	f/22.0	ANGLE OF VIEW H 6.5° / V 4.8° — FIELD OF VIEW
Hyperfocal Distance		115' 4"	80' 9"	57' 8"	40' 4"	28' 10"	20' 2"	14' 8"	10' 1"	7' 4'	
2	NEAR	NA	1' 11"	1' 11"	1' 11"	1' 11"	1' 10"	1' 9"	1' 8"	1' 7"	0' 2.7" x 0' 2"
	FAR	NA	2' 1"	2' 1"	2' 1"	2' 2"	2' 2"	2' 3"	2' 5"	2' 8"	
4	NEAR	3' 10"	3' 10"	3' 9"	3' 8"	3' 6"	3' 4"	3' 2"	2' 11"	2' 8"	0' 5.5" x 0' 4"
	FAR	4' 2"	4' 2"	4' 3"	4' 5"	4' 7"	4' 11"	5' 5"	6' 5"	8' 5"	
6	NEAR	5' 9"	5' 7"	5' 5"	5' 3"	5' 0"	4' 8"	4' 4"	3' 10"	3' 4"	0' 8" x 0' 6"
	FAR	6' 4"	6' 6"	6' 8"	7' 0"	7' 6"	8' 5"	10' 0"	14' 3"	29' 4"	
8	NEAR	7' 6"	7' 4"	7' 1"	6' 8"	6' 3"	5' 9"	5' 3"	4' 6"	3' 10"	0' 11" x 0' 8"
	FAR	8' 7"	8' 10"	9' 3"	9' 11"	11' 0"	13' 1"	17' 2"	35' 10"	INF	
10	NEAR	9' 3"	8' 11"	8' 7"	8' 0"	7' 5"	6' 9"	6' 0"	5' 1"	4' 3"	1' 2.6" x 0' 10"
	FAR	10' 11"	11' 5"	12' 1"	13' 3"	15' 2"	19' 6"	30' 4"	INF	INF	
12	NEAR	10' 11"	10' 6"	9' 11"	9' 3"	8' 6"	7' 7"	6' 8"	5' 6"	4' 7"	1' 4" x 1' 0"
	FAR	13' 4"	14' 1"	15' 1"	17' 0"	20' 4"	29' 0"	62' 0"	INF	INF	
16	NEAR	14' 1"	13' 5"	12' 7"	11' 6"	10' 4"	9' 0"	7' 8"	6' 3"	5' 1"	1' 10" x 1' 4"
	FAR	18' 7"	19' 11"	22' 1"	26' 4"	35' 6"	74' 4"	INF	INF	INF	
25	NEAR	20' 7"	19' 1"	17' 6"	15' 6"	13' 5"	11' 2"	9' 3"	7' 3"	5' 8"	2' 10" x 2' 1"
	FAR	31' 10"	36' 1"	43' 11"	65' 0"	180' 5"	INF	INF	INF	INF	

84

VERTICAL ANGLE VS. EFFECTIVE FOCAL LENGTH
(Focal Length In Millimeters)

TRANSMITTED OR PROJECTED IMAGE	0.189"	0.260"	0.375"	0.500"	0.158"	0.286"	0.251"	0.446"	0.594"	0.700"	0.991"	0.870"
ANGLE (DEGREES)	TV 1/2" CCD	TV 2/3" CCD	TV 1" CCD	TV 1 2/3" CCD	SUPER -8	16mm	SUPER -16 1.85:1 AR	35mm 1.85:1 AR	35mm TV TRANS	35mm ANA	35mm VISTA	65mm
0.5	550	757	1091	1445	460	832	731	1298	1729	2037	2884	2532
0.7	393	541	780	1039	328	595	522	927	1235	1455	2060	1809
1	275	378	546	728	230	416	365	649	864	1019	1442	1266
1.5	183	252	364	485	153	277	244	433	576	679	961	844
2	138	189	273	364	115	280	183	325	432	509	721	633
2.5	110	151	218	291	92	166	146	260	346	407	577	506
3	92	126	182	242	77	139	122	216	288	339	481	422
3.5	79	108	156	208	66	119	104	185	247	291	412	362
4	69	95	136	182	57	104	91	162	216	256	360	316
4.5	61	84	121	162	51	92	81	144	192	226	320	281
5	55	76	109	145	46	83	73	130	173	204	288	253
6	46	63	91	121	38	69	61	108	144	170	240	211
7	39	54	78	104	33	59	52	93	123	145	206	181
8	34	47	68	91	29	52	46	81	108	127	180	158
9	30	42	61	81	25	46	41	72	96	113	160	140
10	27	38	54	73	23	42	36	65	86	102	144	126
15	18	25	36	48	15	28	24	43	57	68	96	84
20	14	19	27	36	11	21	18	32	43	50	71	63
25	11	15	21	29	9	16	14	26	34	40	57	50
30	9	12	18	24	7	14	12	21	28	33	47	41
35	8	10	15	20	6	12	10	18	24	28	40	35
40	7	9	13	17	6	10	9	16	21	24	35	30
45	6	8	11	15	5	9	8	14	18	21	30	27
50	5	7	10	14	4	8	7	12	16	19	27	24
55	5	6	9	12	4	7	6	11	15	17	24	21
60	4	6	8	11	3	6	6	10	13	15	22	19
65	4	5	7	10	3	6	5	9	12	14	20	17
70	3	5	7	9	3	5	5	8	11	13	18	16
75	3	4	6	8	3	5	4	7	10	12	16	14
80	3	4	6	8	2	4	4	7	9	11	15	13
85	3	4	5	7	2	4	3	6	8	10	14	12
90	2	3	5	6	2	4	3	6	8	9	13	11
95	2	3	4	6	2	3	3	5	7	8	12	10
100	2	3	4	5	2	3	3	5	6	7	11	9

HORIZONTAL ANGLE VS. EFFECTIVE FOCAL LENGTH
(Focal Length In Millimeters)

TRANSMITTED OR PROJECTED IMAGE	0.252"	0.346"	0.5"	0.667"	0.209"	0.380"	0.463"	0.825"	1.676"	1.485"	1.912"
ANGLE (DEGREES)	TV ½" CCD	TV ⅔" CCD	TV 1" CCD	TV 1⅔" CCD	SUPER -8	16mm	SUPER -16 1.85:1 AR	35mm 1.85:1 AR	35mm ANA	35mm VISTA	65mm
0.5	733	1007	1455	1941	608	1106	1348	2401	4878	4322	5565
0.7	524	719	1039	1387	435	790	963	1715	3484	3087	3975
1	367	504	728	971	304	553	674	1201	2439	2161	2782
1.5	244	336	485	647	203	369	449	800	1626	1441	1855
2	183	252	364	485	152	276	337	600	1219	1081	1391
2.5	147	201	291	388	122	221	269	480	975	864	1113
3	122	168	242	323	101	184	225	400	813	720	927
3.5	105	144	208	277	87	158	192	343	697	617	795
4	92	126	182	243	76	138	168	300	610	540	695
4.5	81	112	162	216	68	123	150	267	542	480	618
5	73	101	145	194	61	111	135	240	488	432	556
6	61	84	121	162	51	92	112	200	406	360	463
7	52	72	104	138	43	79	96	171	348	308	397
8	46	63	91	121	38	69	84	150	304	270	347
9	41	56	81	108	34	61	75	133	270	240	309
10	37	50	73	97	30	55	67	120	243	216	278
15	24	33	45	64	20	37	45	80	162	143	184
20	18	25	36	48	15	27	33	59	121	107	138
25	14	20	29	38	12	22	27	47	96	85	110
30	12	16	24	32	10	18	22	39	79	70	91
35	10	14	20	27	8	15	19	33	68	60	77
40	9	12	17	23	7	13	16	29	58	52	67
45	8	11	15	20	6	12	14	25	51	46	59
50	7	9	14	18	6	10	13	22	46	40	52
55	6	8	12	16	5	9	11	20	41	36	47
60	6	8	11	15	5	8	10	18	37	33	42
65	5	7	10	13	4	8	9	16	33	30	38
70	5	6	9	12	4	7	8	15	30	27	35
75	4	6	8	11	3	6	8	14	28	25	32
80	4	5	8	10	3	6	7	12	25	22	29
85	3	5	7	9	3	5	6	11	23	21	26
90	3	4	6	8	3	5	6	10	21	19	24
95	3	4	6	8	2	4	5	10	20	17	22
100	3	4	5	7	2	4	5	9	18	16	20

PLUS DIOPTER LENSES
FOCUS CONVERSION TABLE
16mm or 35mm Camera

(MAY BE USED WITH ANY FOCAL LENGTH LENS)

NOTE: Position diopter lens in front of camera lens so that arrow (if inscribed on rim) points toward subject., or with convex (outward) curve toward subject. When two diopters are used in combination, place highest power nearest camera lens. The acutual field size photographed depends slightly on the separation between diopter and camera lens.

Power of Supplementary Lens in Diopters	Focusing Distance on Lens Mount in FEET	Actual Distance Focused on in INCHES From Diopter Lens
$+\frac{1}{4}$	Inf.	157 $\frac{1}{2}$
	25	139
	15	129 $\frac{1}{2}$
	10	118 $\frac{1}{2}$
	6	102
	4	86 $\frac{1}{2}$
$+\frac{1}{2}$	Inf.	78 $\frac{3}{4}$
	25	69 $\frac{1}{2}$
	15	64 $\frac{3}{4}$
	10	59 $\frac{1}{4}$
	6	51
	4	43 $\frac{1}{4}$
$+1$	Inf.	39 $\frac{3}{8}$
	25	34 $\frac{3}{8}$
	15	32 $\frac{3}{8}$
	10	29 $\frac{5}{8}$
	6	25 $\frac{1}{2}$
	4	21 $\frac{5}{8}$
$+2$	Inf.	19 $\frac{5}{8}$
	25	18 $\frac{1}{2}$
	15	17 $\frac{3}{3}$
	10	16 $\frac{7}{8}$
	6	15 $\frac{1}{2}$
	4	14
$+3$ (2+1)	Inf.	13 $\frac{1}{8}$
	25	12 $\frac{1}{2}$
	15	12 $\frac{1}{4}$
	10	11 $\frac{7}{8}$
	6	11 $\frac{1}{8}$
	4	10 $\frac{3}{8}$
+4	Inf.	9 $\frac{7}{8}$
+5	Inf.	7 $\frac{7}{8}$
+6	Inf.	6 $\frac{1}{2}$
+8	Inf.	5
+10	Inf.	4

EASTMAN KODAK — Color Negative Films

Color Negative	Balance	Emulsion Type 35mm/16mm	Edge	EI			
				T	filter	D	filter
Kodak Vision3 200T	T	5213/7213	EO	200	–	125	85
Kodak Vision3 250D	D	5207/7207	EN	64	80A	250	–
Kodak Vision3 50D	D	5203/7203	ER	12	80A	50	–
Kodak Vision3 500T	T	5219/7219	EJ	500	–	320	85
Kodak 500T	T	5230/7230	EZ	500	-	320	85

All stocks also available in 65mm.
All print stocks are 70mm. All camera stocks are 65mm

APPROXIMATE WARM-UP TIME FOR FILM PACKAGES

Difference between room temperature and refrigerator temperature	14°C (25°F) Rise		55°C (100°F) Rise	
Relative humidity in room	70%	90%	70%	90%
Warm-up time (hours)				
Single Super-8mm roll	½	1	1	1½
Single 16mm roll	½	1	1	1½
Single 35mm roll	1½	3	3	5
Carton of ten 35mm rolls	12	28	30	46

Damage from moisture occurs when you remove the film can from cold storage and do not allow sufficient warm-up time before you remove the seal. Example: For each 14°C (25°F) of temperature rise for a single 16mm roll at 70% humidity allow ½ hour.

EASTMAN KODAK — Color Reversal Films

Color Reversal	Balance	Emulsion Type 35mm\16mm	Edge	EI			
				T	filter	D	filter
Kodak Ektachrome 100D	D	5285/7285	EA	25	80A	100	—

EASTMAN KODAK — Black-and-White Negative Films

B&W Negative	Emulsion Type 35mm/16mm	Edge	EI	
			T	D
Eastman Double-X	5222/7222	E	200	250

EASTMAN KODAK — Black-and-White Reversal Films

B&W Reversal	Emulsion Type 16mm	Edge	EI	
			T	D
Kodak Tri-X Reversal	7266 (16mm only)	ED	160	200
	*in manually operated & automatic Super 8 cameras		160	160
	*for negative processing in motion picture negative developer		100	125

EASTMAN KODAK — Super 8 Films

Color Negative and Reversal	T	D
Kodak Vision3 (7213) 200T	200	125 (with an 85 filter)
Kodak Vision3 (7219) 500T	500	320 (with an 85 filter)
Kodak Ektachrome (7285) 100D	25 (with an 80A filter)	100
Black and White Reversal	T	D
Tri-X Reversal (7266)	160	200

EASTMAN KODAK — Laboratory Films

Color Print Film	Emulsion Type 35mm/16mm
Kodak Vision Premier Color Print Film	2393 (35mm only)
Kodak Vision Color Print Film	2383

Black and White Print Film	Emulsion Type 35mm/16mm
Eastman Fine Grain Release Positive Film	5302/7302
Kodak Black and White Print Film	2302/3302

Color Intermediate Films	Emulsion Type 35mm/16mm
Kodak Vision Color Intermediate Film	2242/3242
Kodak Vision Color Internegative II Film	2273/5273/7273/3273
Kodak Vision3 Color Digital Intermediate Film	2254

Black and White Intermediate Films	Emulsion Type 35mm/16mm
Kodak Vision Fine Grain Duplicating Positive Film	2366/3366
Kodak Vision Fine Grain Duplicating Panchromatic Negative Film	2234/5234/7234/3234
Kodak Vision High Contrast Panchromatic Film	2369
Kodak Vision High Contrast Positive Film II	5363/7363
Kodak Vision Panchromatic Separation Film	2238 (35mm and 65mm only)

Sound Film	Emulsion Type 35mm/16mm
Kodak Panchromatic Sound Recording Film	2374/3374
Eastman EXR Sound Recording Film	2378/3378

FUJI Film — Color Negative Films

Color Negative	Balance	Emulsion Type 35mm/16mm	Edge	ASA\ISO			
				T	filter	D	filter
ETERNA VIVID 500	T	8547/8647	FN47	500	–	320	85
ETERNA 500	T	8573/8673	FN73	500	–	320	85
REALA 500D	D	8592/8692	FN92	125	80A	500	–
ETERNA 400	T	8583/8683	FN83	400	–	250	85
ETERNA 250	T	8553/8653	FN53	250	–	160	85
ETERNA VIVID 250	T	8546/8646	FN46	250	–	160	85
ETERNA 250D	D	8563/8663	FN63	64	80A	250	–
ETERNA VIVID 160	T	8543/8643	FN43	160	–	100	85
F-125	T	8532/8632	N32	125	–	80	85
F-64D	D	8522/8622	N22	16	80A	64	–

FUJI Film — Laboratory Films

Color print film	Emulsion Type 35mm/16mm
Fujicolor positive film ETERNA	3512/3612 (not available in U.S.) 3514DI/3614DI
	3523XD (35mm, higher contrast film, available in U.S. only)
Black-and-White Print Film	**Emulsion Type 35mm**
Panchromatic High-Con, fine grain positive film	71337
Color Intermediate Films	**Emulsion Type 35mm**
ETERNA RDI (for digital intermediates)	8511 (acetate base)
	4511 (estar base)
ETERNA CI	8503 (acetate base)
	4503 (estar base)
Black-and-White Recording Film	**Emulsion Type 35mm**
ETERNA RDS (for digital separations)	4791 (estar base)

FILM WEIGHT IN CANS

16mm	35mm
100 ft. = 3 ¼ oz. (200 grams) 400 ft. = 1 lb. (500 grams)	400 ft. = 2 lbs. 3 oz. (1 Kg.) 1000 ft. = 5 lbs. 8 oz. (2.5 Kg.)

65mm	
1000 ft. = 10 lbs. (4.54 Kg.)	

Selected Color Filters for B&W Cinematography Daylight Exteriors

Kodak Wratten #	Color		Effect/Use	Average Exposure Factor	T/stop Increase
3	Light Yellow		Slight Correction	1.5	$2/3$
8	Yellow		Corrects color rendition to visual appearance as gray	2	1
12	Deep Yellow		Slight over correction. Useful in aerial cinematography	2.5 (Reversal Film 2)	$1\ 1/3$ (1)
15	Deep Yellow		Greater contrast. Useful with the tele lenses and for aerial cinematography	3	$1\ 2/3$
21	Orange		Same but stronger than #15. Makes blue water dark	3.5 (Reversal Film 3)	$1\ 5/6$ ($1\ 2/3$)
23A	Light Red		Moderate over correction. Not for close ups–whitens faces	5	$2\ 1/3$
25	Red		Very dark sky. Day-for-Night. (complete red separation). No faces!	8 (Reversal film 10)	3 ($3\ 1/3$)
29	Deep Red		Black sky, greenery. Day-for-Night. No faces!	25 (Reversal film 40)	$4\ 2/3$ ($5\ 1/3$)
11	Yellowish Green		Similar to #8 but better flesh tones and flower colors	2	1
56	Light Green		Darkens sky, lightens foliage	4	2
58	Green		(Complete green separation) Lightens dark foliage, darkens sky	6	$2\ 2/3$
47	Blue		(Complete blue separation) Accentuates haze. Darkens reds, Lightens blues	5	$2\ 1/3$
23A + 56			Helps flesh renditions for Day-for-Night. Darkens sky	Day-for-Night 6	$2\ 2/3$
POLA	Gray		Darkens sky, removes reflections.	2.5 to 4	$1\ 1/3$ to 2

Vertical note spanning rows 3–29: From 3 to 29 – renders blue skies increasingly darker and increasingly misty sky. Yellow & Red will not darken a misty sky. From 3 to 29 – penetrates haze.

Color Filters for Altering B&W Contrast of Colored Subjects

Kodak Wratten #	Color of Subject				Tungsten Exposure	
	Blue	Green	Yellow	Red	Factor	T/stop Increase
3	Very Slightly Darker	Very Slightly Lighter	Very Slightly Lighter	Very Slightly Lighter	NR	NR
8	Slightly Darker	Very Slightly Lighter	Slightly Lighter	Very Slightly Lighter	1.5	$2/3$
12	Fairly Dark	Fairly Light	Light	Fairly Light	1.5	$2/3$
15	Dark	Light	Very Light	Light	2	1
21	Dark	Very Slightly Darker	Very Light	Very Light	4	2
23A	Very Dark	Dark	Slightly Lighter	Very Light	3	$1\ 2/3$
25	Black	Very Dark	Fairly Light	Very Light	6	$2\ 2/3$
29	Black	Black	Very Light	White	4	2
11	Fairly Dark	Light	Fairly Light	Medium Dark	3	$1\ 2/3$
56	Fairly Dark	Fairly Light	Slightly Light	Fairly Dark	6	$2\ 2/3$
58	Very Dark	Very Light	Light	Very Dark	8	3
47	White	Dark	Very Dark	Black	8	3
23A + 56	Very Dark	Very Dark	White	Light	NR	NR

Note: Relative to a neutral gray subject, any given filter will render its own color lighter and its complimentary color darker.

Correlated Color Temperature of Typical Light Sources

Artificial Light

Source		Mireds
Match flame	1700°K	588
Candle flame	1850°K	541
Tungsten-gas filled lamps		
40-100W	2650-2900°K	317-345
200-500W	2980°K	336
1000W	2990°K	334

Daylight

Source		Mireds
Sunlight		
Sunrise or sunset	2000°K	500
One hour after sunrise	3500°K	286
Early morning, late afternoon	4300°K	233
Average noon, (Wash. D.C.)	5400°K	185
Midsummer	5800°K	172
Overcast sky	6000°K	167
Average summer daylight	6500°K	154
Light summer shade	7100°K	141
Average summer shade	8000°K	125
Partly cloudy sky	8000-10000°K	125-100
Summer skylight	9500-30000°K	105-33

Sunlight should not be confused with daylight. Sunlight is the light of the sun only. Daylight is a combination of sunlight and skylight. These values are approximate since many factors affect the correlated color temperature. For consistency, 5500°K is considered to be nominal photographic daylight. The difference between 5000°K and 6000°K is only 33 mireds, the same photographic or visual difference as that between household tungsten lights and 3200°K photolamps (the approximate equivalent of ¼ Blue or ⅛ Orange lighting filters).

The MIRED System

When working with sunlight and incandescent sources, the MIRED system offers a convenient means for dealing with problems of measurement when adjusting from one color temperature to another.

Filters which change the effective color temperature of a source by a definite amount can be characterized by a "MIRED shift value." This value is computed as follows:

$$\text{MIRED shift values} = \left(\left[\frac{10^6}{T_2} \right] - \left[\frac{10^6}{T_1} \right] \right)$$

T_1 = kelvin temperature of the original source

T_2 = kelvin temperature of the original source as measured through the filter

Example: What is the MIRED change from 5500°K to 3200°K?

$$T_1 = 5500°K \qquad T_2 = 3200°K$$

$$\frac{1,000,000}{3200} - \frac{1,000,000}{5500}$$

312.5 - 181.8 = 130.7 (rounded to +131)

MIRED shift values can be positive (yellowish or minus blue filters) or negative (blue or minus red/green filters). The same filter (representing a single MIRED shift value) applied on light sources with different color temperatures will produce significantly different color-temperature shifts.   SSF

Kodak Conversion Filters for Color Films

Filter Color	Filter Number	Exposure Increase In Stops*	Conversion In Degrees °K	Mired Shift Value
Blue	80A	2	3200 to 5500°K	-131
	80B	1 ²/₃	3400 to 5500°K	-112
	80C	1	3800 to 5500°K	-81
	80D	¹/₃	4200 to 5500°K	-56
Amber	85C	¹/₃	5500 to 3800°K	+81
	85	²/₃	5500 to 3400°K	+112
	85N3	1 ²/₃	5500 to 3400°K	+112
	85N6	2 ²/₃	5500 to 3400°K	+112
	85N9	3 ²/₃	5500 to 3400°K	+112
	85B	²/₃	5500 to 3200°K	+131

*These values are approximate. For critical work, they should be checked by practical test, especially if more than one filter is used.

Kodak Light Balancing Filters

Filter Color	Filter Number	Exposure Increase In Stops*	To Obtain 3200 °K From:	To Obtain 3400 °K From:	Mired Shift Value
Bluish	82C + 82C	1 ¹/₃	2490°K	2610°K	-89
	82C + 82B	1 ¹/₃	2570°K	2700°K	-77
	82C + 82A	1	2650°K	2780°K	-65
	82C + 82	1	2720°K	2870°K	-55
	82C	²/₃	2800°K	2950°K	-45
	82B	²/₃	2900°K	3060°K	-32
	82A	¹/₃	3000°K	3180°K	-21
	82	¹/₃	3100°K	3290°K	-10
	No Filter Necessary		3200 °K	3400 °K	
Yellowish	81	¹/₃	3300°K	3510°K	+9
	81A	¹/₃	3400°K	3630°K	+18
	81B	¹/₃	3500°K	3740°K	+27
	81C	¹/₃	3600°K	3850°K	+35
	81D	²/₃	3700°K	3970°K	+42
	81EF	²/₃	3850°K	4140°K	+52

*These values are approximate. For critical work, they should be checked by practical test, especially if more than one filter is used.

Kodak Color Compensating Filters for Color Films

Peak Density	Yellow (Absorbs Blue)	Exposure Increase In Stops*	Magenta (Absorbs Green)	Exposure Increase In Stops*	Cyan (Absorbs Red)	Exposure Increase In Stops*
.05	CC-05Y	$\frac{1}{6}$	CC-05M	$\frac{1}{3}$	CC-05C	$\frac{1}{3}$
.10	CC-10Y	$\frac{1}{3}$	CC-10M	$\frac{1}{3}$	CC-10C	$\frac{1}{3}$
.20	CC-20Y	$\frac{1}{3}$	CC-20M	$\frac{1}{3}$	CC-20C	$\frac{1}{3}$
.30	CC-30Y	$\frac{1}{3}$	CC-30M	$\frac{2}{3}$	CC-30C	$\frac{2}{3}$
.40	CC-40Y	$\frac{1}{3}$	CC-40M	$\frac{2}{3}$	CC-40C	$\frac{2}{3}$
.50	CC-50Y	$\frac{2}{3}$	CC-50M	$\frac{2}{3}$	CC-50C	1

Peak Density	Red (Absorbs Blue and Green)	Exposure Increase In Stops*	Green (Absorbs Blue and Red)	Exposure Increase In Stops*	Blue (Absorbs Red and Green)	Exposure Increase In Stops*
.05	CC-05R	$\frac{1}{3}$	CC-05G	$\frac{1}{3}$	CC-05B	$\frac{1}{3}$
.10	CC-10R	$\frac{1}{3}$	CC-10G	$\frac{1}{3}$	CC-10B	$\frac{1}{3}$
.20	CC-20R	$\frac{1}{3}$	CC-20G	$\frac{1}{3}$	CC-20B	$\frac{2}{3}$
.30	CC-30R	$\frac{2}{3}$	CC-30G	$\frac{2}{3}$	CC-30B	$\frac{2}{3}$
.40	CC-40R	$\frac{2}{3}$	CC-40G	$\frac{2}{3}$	CC-40B	1
.50	CC-50R	1	CC-50G	1	CC-50B	$1\frac{1}{3}$

* These values are approximate. For critical work, they should be checked by practical test, especially if more than one filter is used.

Kodak Ultraviolet and Haze Cutting Filters

Kodak Wratten #	Color	Effect/Use (no exposure increase required)
1A (skylight)	Pale Pink	Absorbs ultraviolet for color film. To reduce blue outdoors in open shade under clear blue sky.
2A	Pale Yellow	Absorbs ultraviolet below 405nm. Reduces haze in black-and-white film.
2B	Pale Yellow	Absorbs ultraviolet below 390nm. More effective than 2A in haze reduction.
2C	Pale Yellow	Absorbs ultraviolet below 385nm. Less effective than 2B in haze reduction.
2E	Pale Yellow	Absorbs ultaviolet below 415nm. Similar to 2B, but absorbs more violet.
HF-3	Light Yellow	Haze cutting filter for aerial photography.
HF-4	Very Light Yellow	Haze cutting filter. Always used in combination with HF-3 filter. For color balancing of different sky conditions and altitudes.
HF-5	Very Light Yellow	Haze cutting filter. Always used in combination with HF-3 filter. For color balancing of different sky conditions and altitudes.

TYPICAL DEEP DYED POLYESTER FILTERS FOR LAMP COLOR CORRECTION

Filter Names	BLUE (CTB)		ORANGE (CTO)		CC EQUIVALENT	
	Effect on 3200°K (312 MIRED)	MIRED Shift Value	Effect on 5500°K (182 MIRED)	MIRED Shift Value	Plus Green	Minus Green (magenta)
Full	5500°K	– 131	3200°K	+ 131	CC30G	CC30M
¾	4720°K	– 100	3436°K	+ 124	–	–
½	4100°K	– 68	3440°K	+ 109	CC15G	CC15M
¼	3610°K	– 35	4660°K	+ 64	CC075G	CC075M
⅛	3330°K	– 12	4600°K	+ 26	CC035G	CC035M

Varies by manufacturer. Must use color temperature meter for accuracy.

SSC

COLOR BALANCING TO MATCH DAYLIGHT OR AMBIENT LIGHT ON LOCATION INTERIORS

Emulsion Balance	Exposure Balance	Camera Filter	Photographic Lights/Filters	Practical Existing Lights/Filters	Window Filters
BALANCING INTERIOR TO DAYLIGHT FROM WINDOWS					
3200°K	Daylight	85Neg 85B Rev.	**3200°K Tungsten/** Full Blue CTB or Dichroic	**Household Tungsten/** Full Blue + ¼ CTB	ND as required
			White flame Arc/Y-1		
			HMI, CID/Y-1	See pp 99 for Fluorescent, Mercury and Sodium Vapor Lamps	
			5500°K Kino Flo GE Cinema55/None		
Daylight	Daylight	None	Use same filters as above		
BALANCING COLOR OF AMBIENT LIGHTING TO 3200°K					
3200°K	3200°K	None	**3200°K Tungsten/** None	**Household Tungsten/** ¼ CTB	Full or ¾ CTO or Sun 85 plus ND as required
			3200°K HMI/ None		
			3200°K Kino Flo, GE Cinema32/None	See pp 99 for Fluorescent, Mercury and Sodium Vapor Lamps	
			Yellow Flame Arc/YF 101		
			HMI, CID, White Flame Arc/ Y-1+MT2* or MTY or ¾ CTO		
Daylight	3200°K	80A	Use same filters as above		

Exact conversion requires both source and filter to be precise. Artificial daylight sources vary greatly in their ability to replicate photographic daylight (5500°K). White-Flame Carbon Arcs and Xenon lamps are very stable and excellent continuous-spectrum photographic daylight sources. HMI and CID sources are problematic. There can be variations in green output and they tend to lose one degree of Kelvin per hour of lamp life. The consistency in manufacturing of these globes is a factor that requires checking. Even so-called "full-spectrum color-correct" fluorescents will have excess green when they overheat. 3200°K Tungsten-Halogen photographic globes are very stable and have excellent color rendering when operated at 117–120V throughout their life. Filtering systems and LED units vary by manufacturer. They must be checked by a color-temperature meter for accuracy.

Color Balancing for Existing Non-Photographic Lighting

Common Fluorescent and AC Discharge Commercial Lighting	Using existing fluorescent lighting unfiltered								Filtering fluorescent lights to match photo lamps			
	Camera filters (Kodak or equivalent)				Photo lamp filters to match Fluorescent Lamps (Rosco, Lee, Gam or Formatt)				Camera filter: none (Tungsten negative Or reversal)		Camera filter: Tungsten Negative: #85 Daylight film: none	
	3200°K film (Tungsten)	S.I.*	5500°K film (Daylight)	S.I.*	3200°K	L.L.*	5500°K	L.L.*	To match 3200°K	L.L.*	To match 5500°K	L.L.*
Cool white	CC10M +#85	1⅓	CC20M	⅓	Full blue CTB +Plusgreen +Quarter Blue +¼ Plusgreen	3	Plusgreen +Third blue	1	Fluorofilter +½ Minusgreen	1	Minusgreen	⅔
Cool white deluxe	CC10R +#85C	⅔	#82C	⅔	Half blue +¼ Plusgreen +Eighth Blue	1⅓	MT54 +Eighth Blue +UV Filter	1	Sun ½ CTO +¼ Minusgreen +Quarter Blue	1⅓	Quarter blue +¼ Minusgreen +Eighth Blue	1
Warm white	CC30M +#81EF	1⅓	CC50B +CC15M	1⅔	Half Blue +Plusgreen +Quarter blue	2	Plusgreen +½ Plusgreen +Sun ⅛ CTO	1	Minusgreen +¼ Minusgreen +Sun ¼ CTO	1½	Half blue +Minusgreen +Eighth blue	2
Warm white deluxe	CC10M +#81	⅔	#80B +CC05G	2	¼ Plusgreen +Quarter blue +UV Filter	⅔	Sun ½ CTO +UV Filter	⅓	¼ Minusgreen	⅓	Full blue CTB +½ Minusgreen	2⅓
Mercury vapor	CC50M + #85	1⅓	CC50M + #81A	1	½ to Full CTO + 2x to 3x Minusgreen	3⅔ to 2⅓	Full CTB + 2x to 3x Plusgreen	3 to 2⅓	NR		NR	
Sodium vapor	CC30 to 50M +#80A	2 ⅔	CC30M + #80A	2 ⅔	¾ CTO + 101 Yellow	1⅓	1½ to 2x Full CTO + 101 Yellow	2½ to 1⅔	NR		NR	

Check with color temperature meter. *S. I. = Stop Increase *L.L. = Light Loss in stops

Incident Key Light/T-Stop
(Foot Candles)

EI/ASA	2000	1600	1250	1000	800	640	500	400	320
T-stop 1.4	1.25	1.5	2	2.5	3	4	5	6	8
1.6	1.5	2	2.5	3	4	5	6	8	10
1.8	2	2.5	3	4	5	6	8	10	12
2	2.5	3	4	5	6	8	10	12	16
2.2	3	4	5	6	8	10	12	16	20
2.5	4	5	6	8	10	12	16	20	25
2.8	5	6	8	10	12	16	20	25	32
3.2	6	8	10	12	16	20	25	32	40
3.5	8	10	12	16	20	25	32	40	50
4	10	12	16	20	25	32	40	50	64
4.5	12	16	20	25	32	40	50	64	80
5	16	20	25	32	40	50	64	80	100
5.6	20	25	32	40	50	64	80	100	125
6.3	25	32	40	50	64	80	100	125	160
7	32	40	50	64	80	100	125	160	200
8	40	50	64	80	100	125	160	200	250
9	50	64	80	100	125	160	200	250	320
10	64	80	100	125	160	200	250	320	400
11	80	100	125	160	200	250	320	400	500
12.7	100	125	160	200	250	320	400	500	650
14	125	160	200	250	320	400	500	650	800
16	160	200	250	320	400	500	650	800	1000
18	200	250	320	400	500	650	800	1000	1290
20	250	320	400	500	650	800	1000	1290	1625
22	320	400	500	650	800	1000	1290	1625	2050

Most cinematography is at 24 frames per second. The table is calculated for foot candles incident light on a fully lighted subject at ⅕₀ second exposure (172.8° precisely, but 170° to 180° varies from this by less than a printer point for normally processed color negative). For photography at ⅙₀ second (30 frames per second, 180° shutter; or 24 frames per second, 144° shutter), use one-third wider lens stop or one column to the right (one ASA step lower) on the incident light table.

Incident Key Light/T-Stop
(Foot Candles)

EI/ASA	250	200	160	125	100	80	64	50	40
T-stop 1.4	10	12	16	20	25	32	40	50	64
1.6	12	16	20	25	32	40	50	64	80
1.8	16	20	25	32	40	50	64	80	100
2	20	25	32	40	50	64	80	100	125
2.2	25	32	40	50	64	80	100	125	160
2.5	32	40	50	64	80	100	125	160	200
2.8	40	50	64	80	100	125	160	200	250
3.2	50	64	80	100	125	160	200	250	320
3.5	64	80	100	125	160	200	250	320	400
4	80	100	125	160	200	250	320	400	500
4.5	100	125	160	200	250	320	400	500	650
5	125	160	200	250	320	400	500	650	800
5.6	160	200	250	320	400	500	650	800	1000
6.3	200	250	320	400	500	650	800	1000	1290
7	250	320	400	500	650	800	1000	1290	1625
8	320	400	500	650	800	1000	1290	1625	2050
9	400	500	650	800	1000	1290	1625	2050	2580
10	500	650	800	1000	1290	1625	2050	2580	3250
11	650	800	1000	1290	1625	2050	2580	3250	4100
12.7	800	1000	1290	1625	2050	2580	3250	4100	5160
14	1000	1290	1625	2050	2580	3250	4100	5160	6500
16	1290	1625	2050	2580	3250	4100	5160	6500	8200
18	1625	2050	2580	3250	4100	5160	6500	8200	10000
20	2050	2580	3250	4100	5160	6500	8200	10000	
22	2580	3250	4100	5160	6500	8200	10000		

COMPARISON OF LIGHT VALUES
1 Footcandle = 10.764 Lux
1 Lux = .0929 Footcandles
1 Foot Lambert = 3.426 candelas per square meter
1 Candela per square meter = .292 Foot Lamberts

Incident Key Light/T-Stop
(Foot Candles)

EI/ASA	32	25	20	16	12	10	8	6
T-stop 1.4	80	100	125	160	200	250	320	400
1.6	100	125	160	200	250	320	400	500
1.8	125	160	200	250	320	400	500	650
2	160	200	250	320	400	500	650	800
2.2	200	250	320	400	500	650	800	1000
2.5	250	320	400	500	650	800	1000	1290
2.8	320	400	500	650	800	1000	1290	1625
3.2	400	500	650	800	1000	1290	1625	2050
3.5	500	650	800	1000	1290	1625	2050	2580
4	650	800	1000	1290	1625	2050	2580	3250
4.5	800	1000	1290	1625	2050	2580	3250	4100
5	1000	1290	1625	2050	2580	3250	4100	5160
5.6	1290	1625	2050	2580	3250	4100	5160	6500
6.3	1625	2050	2580	3250	4100	5160	6500	8200
7	2050	2580	3250	4100	5160	6500	8200	10,000
8	2580	3250	4100	5160	6500	8200	10,000	
9	3250	4100	5160	6500	8200	10,000		
10	4100	5160	6500	8200	10,000			
11	5160	6500	8200	10,000				
12.7	6500	8200	10,000					
14	8200	10,000						
16	10,000							
18								
20								
22								

1 Foot Lambert = .31831 Candelas per square foot
1 Foot Lambert = .0010764 Lamberts
1 Foot Lambert = 1 Lumen per square foot
1 Lumen = .07958 Candle Power (spherical)
1 Lumen = .00015 Watts

AC Arc Lamp Flicker Problem

Lamps that can exhibit flicker problems include fluorescents, mercury vapor, metal halide additive types and high-pressure sodium, as well as, photographic types such as HMI, CID or low-pressure AC Xenon arcs.

All of the lamps listed require the use of a ballasting system to provide current limiting after the arc is struck. In the past few years, an increasing number of reliable, electronic "flicker-free" 25,000 Hz ballasts have become available for HMI and some fluorescent wattages. However, a significant number of inductive (magnetic) ballasts are still around.

The time related factors involved in ensuring a uniform exposure from frame to frame using these types of light sources (i.e., flicker-free) are the following:

1. Stability of the power frequency to lamp ballast
2. Camera frame rate
3. Stability of camera speed (crystal control)
4. Camera shutter angle (ideal for 60 Hz 144°, 50 Hz 172.8°)
5. Phase of shutter relative to light (particularly at high camera speed)

For 60Hz power, the only valid speeds are any that can divide into 120 evenly (e.g. 1, 2, 3, 4, 5, 6, 8, 10, 12, 15, 20, 24, 30, 40, 60, 120fps). For 50 Hz power, the shutter speed must divide into 100 evenly (e.g. 1, 2, 4, 5, 10, 20, 25, 50, 100fps). At these speeds, any shutter angle maybe used.

SSF

Ohm's Law

Amps = watts ÷ voltage, Voltage = watts ÷ amps, and Watts = voltage x amps. Example: 1000watts divided by 120 volts = 8.3amps.

SSF

Shutter Angle / f.p.s. / T-stop change
(for 24 or 30 f.p.s. projection)

f.p.s.	24	22	20	19	18	16	15	14	12	9.5	7.6	6.	4.8(5)	3.8(4)	3	2.4
f.p.s.	30	27	25	24	22	20	19	17	15	12	9.5	7.6	6.	5(4.8)	4(3.8)	3
Exposure change in T-stops	0			⅓			⅔		1	1⅓	1⅔	2	2⅓	2⅔	3	3⅓
Maximum Shutter 235°	235°	215°	196°	**188°**	176°	157°	**147°**	137°	**118°**	**93°**	**74°**	**59°**	**47°**	**37°**	**29°**	**24°**
200	200	183°	167°	**158°**	150°	133°	**125°**	117°	**100°**	**79°**	**63°**	**50°**	**40°**	**32°**	**25°**	**20°**
180	180	165°	150°	**143°**	135°	120°	**113°**	105°	**90°**	**71°**	**57°**	**45°**	**36°**	**29°**	**23°**	**18°**
170	170	156°	142°	**135°**	128°	113°	**106°**	99°	**85°**	**67°**	**54°**	**43°**	**34°**	**27°**	**21°**	**17°**
150	150	138°	125°	**119°**	113°	100°	**94°**	88°	**75°**	**59°**	**48°**	**38°**	**30°**	**24°**	**19°**	**15°**
140	140	128°	117°	**111°**	105°	93°	**88°**	82°	**70°**	**55°**	**44°**	**35°**	**28°**	**22°**	**18°**	**14°**
135	135	124°	113°	**107°**	101°	90°	**84°**	79°	**68°**	**53°**	**43°**	**34°**	**27°**	**21°**	**17°**	**14°**

If it is desired to slow the camera without varying the lens stop but maintain constant exposure:

If it is desired to reduce exposure without varying the lens stop:

If it is desired to reduce the exposure time per frame without reducing exposure:

This table gives shutter angles in one-third T-stop exposure intervals (bold columns) as well as for some camera speeds in less than one-third stop intervals.

CAMERA SPEED EXPOSURE COMPENSATOR
Exposure Increase and Decrease
Above And Below Normal 24 F.P.S.

ABOVE NORMAL SPEED		
Frames Per Second	Factor	Stops Increase (open up)
24	0	0
30	1.25	⅓
38	1.5	⅔
48	2	1
60	2.5	1 ⅓
76	3	1 ⅔
96	4	2
120	5	2 ⅓
150	6	2 ⅔
192	8	3
240	10	3 ⅓
300	12	3 ⅔
384	16	4
484	20	4 ⅓

BELOW NORMAL SPEED		
Frames Per Second	Factor	Stops Decrease (close down)
24	0	0
19	1.25	⅓
15	1.5	⅔
12	2	1
9 1/2	2.5	1 ⅓
7 1/2	3	1 ⅔
6	4	2
3	8	3

Super 8mm Footage Table
Running Times and Film Lengths for Common Projection Speeds

	Super 8 (72 frames per foot)			
Projection speed in frames per second	18		24	
Running time and film length	Feet	+ Frames	Feet	+ Frames
Seconds 1	0	18	0	24
2	0	36	0	48
3	0	54	1	0
4	1	0	1	24
5	1	18	1	48
6	1	36	2	0
7	1	54	2	24
8	2	0	2	48
9	2	18	3	0
10	2	36	3	24
20	5	0	6	48
30	7	36	10	0
40	10	0	13	24
50	12	36	16	48
Minutes 1	15	0	20	0
2	30	0	40	0
3	45	0	60	0
4	60	0	80	0
5	75	0	100	0
6	90	0	120	0
7	105	0	140	0
8	120	0	160	0
9	135	0	180	0
10	150	0	200	0
15	225	0	300	0
20	300	0	400	0
30	450	0	600	0

16mm FOOTAGE TABLE — 24 F.P.S.

24 F.P.S. Sound Speed (1 foot = 40 frames)

Seconds			Seconds			Minutes		Minutes	
SECONDS	FEET	FRAMES	SECONDS	FEET	FRAMES	MINUTES	FEET	MINUTES	FEET
1		24	31	18	24	1	36	31	1116
2	1	8	32	19	8	2	72	32	1152
3	1	32	33	19	32	3	108	33	1188
4	2	16	34	20	16	4	144	34	1224
5	3		35	21		5	180	35	1260
6	3	24	36	21	24	6	216	36	1296
7	4	8	37	22	8	7	252	37	1332
8	4	32	38	22	32	8	288	38	1368
9	5	16	39	23	16	9	324	39	1404
10	6	10	40	24		10	360	40	1440
11	6	24	41	24	24	11	396	41	1476
12	7	8	42	25	8	12	432	42	1512
13	7	32	43	25	32	13	468	43	1548
14	8	16	44	26	16	14	504	44	1584
15	9		45	27		15	540	45	1620
16	9	24	46	27	24	16	576	46	1656
17	10	8	47	28	8	17	612	47	1692
18	10	32	48	28	32	18	648	48	1728
19	11	16	49	29	16	19	684	49	1764
20	12		50	30		20	720	50	1800
21	12	24	51	30	24	21	756	51	1836
22	13	8	52	31	8	22	792	52	1872
23	13	32	53	31	32	23	828	53	1908
24	14	16	54	32	16	24	864	54	1944
25	15		55	33		25	900	55	1980
26	15	24	56	33	24	26	936	56	2016
27	16	8	57	34	8	27	972	57	2052
28	16	32	58	34	32	28	1008	58	2088
29	17	16	59	35	16	29	1044	59	2124
30	18		60	36		30	1080	60	2160

35mm FOOTAGE TABLE 24 F.P.S.
24 F.P.S. Sound Speed (1 foot = 16 frames)

	Seconds						Minutes		
SECONDS	FEET	FRAMES	SECONDS	FEET	FRAMES	MINUTES	FEET	MINUTES	FEET
1	1	8	31	46	8	1	90	31	2790
2	3		32	48		2	180	32	2880
3	4	8	33	49	8	3	270	33	2970
4	6		34	51		4	360	34	3060
5	7	8	35	52	8	5	450	35	3150
6	9		36	54		6	540	36	3240
7	10	8	37	55	8	7	630	37	3330
8	12		38	57		8	720	38	3420
9	13	8	39	58	8	9	810	39	3510
10	15		40	60		10	900	40	3600
11	16	8	41	61	8	11	990	41	3690
12	18		42	63		12	1080	42	3780
13	19	8	43	64	8	13	1170	43	3870
14	21		44	66		14	1260	44	3960
15	22	8	45	67	8	15	1350	45	4050
16	24		46	69		16	1440	46	4140
17	25	8	47	70	8	17	1530	47	4230
18	27		48	72		18	1620	48	4320
19	28	8	49	73	8	19	1710	49	4410
20	30		50	75		20	1800	50	4500
21	31	8	51	76	8	21	1890	51	4590
22	33		52	78		22	1980	52	4680
23	34	8	53	79	8	23	2070	53	4770
24	36		54	81		24	2160	54	4860
25	37	8	55	82	8	25	2250	55	4950
26	39		56	84		26	2340	56	5040
27	40	8	57	85	8	27	2430	57	5130
28	42		58	87		28	2520	58	5220
29	43	8	59	88	8	29	2610	59	5310
30	45		60	90		30	2700	60	5400

16mm Frame Totalizer
Showing Amount of Frames in Various Footage Totals of **16mm** Film

$\frac{1}{20}$ foot = 2 frames	$\frac{3}{10}$ foot = 12 frames	$\frac{7}{10}$ foot = 28 frames
$\frac{1}{10}$ foot = 4 frames	$\frac{3}{8}$ foot = 15 frames	$\frac{3}{4}$ foot = 30 frames
$\frac{1}{8}$ foot = 5 frames	$\frac{2}{5}$ foot = 16 frames	$\frac{4}{5}$ foot = 32 frames
$\frac{1}{5}$ foot = 8 frames	$\frac{1}{2}$ foot = 20 frames	$\frac{9}{10}$ foot = 36 frames
$\frac{1}{4}$ foot = 10 frames	$\frac{3}{5}$ foot = 24 frames	1 foot = 40 frames

Feet	Frames	Feet	Frames	Feet	Frames	Feet	Frames	Feet	Frames
1 =	40	21 =	840	41 =	1640	61 =	2440	81 =	3240
2 =	80	22 =	880	42 =	1680	62 =	2480	82 =	3280
3 =	120	23 =	920	43 =	1720	63 =	2520	83 =	3320
4 =	160	24 =	960	44 =	1760	64 =	2560	84 =	3360
5 =	200	25 =	1000	45 =	1800	65 =	2600	85 =	3400
6 =	240	26 =	1040	46 =	1840	66 =	2640	86 =	3440
7 =	280	27 =	1080	47 =	1880	67 =	2680	87 =	3480
8 =	320	28 =	1120	48 =	1920	68 =	2720	88 =	3520
9 =	360	29 =	1160	49 =	1960	69 =	2760	89 =	3560
10 =	400	30 =	1200	50 =	2000	70 =	2800	90 =	3600
11 =	440	31 =	1240	51 =	2040	71 =	2840	91 =	3640
12 =	480	32 =	1280	52 =	2080	72 =	2880	92 =	3680
13 =	520	33 =	1320	53 =	2120	73 =	2920	93 =	3720
14 =	560	34 =	1360	54 =	2160	74 =	2960	94 =	3760
15 =	600	35 =	1400	55 =	2200	75 =	3000	95 =	3800
16 =	640	36 =	1440	56 =	2240	76 =	3040	96 =	3840
17 =	680	37 =	1480	57 =	2280	77 =	3080	97 =	3880
18 =	720	38 =	1520	58 =	2320	78 =	3120	98 =	3920
19 =	760	39 =	1560	59 =	2360	79 =	3160	99 =	3960
20 =	800	40 =	1600	60 =	2400	80 =	3200	100 =	4000

35mm Frame Totalizer
Showing Amount of Frames in Various Footage Totals of **35mm** Film

1/8 foot = 2 frames			5/8 foot = 10 frames		
1/4 foot = 4 frames			3/4 foot = 12 frames		
3/8 foot = 6 frames			7/8 foot = 14 frames		
1/2 foot = 8 frames			1 foot = 16 frames		

Feet	Frames	Feet	Frames	Feet	Frames	Feet	Frames	Feet	Frames
1 =	16	23 =	368	45 =	720	67 =	1072	89 =	1424
2 =	32	24 =	368	46 =	736	68 =	1088	90 =	1440
3 =	48	25 =	400	47 =	752	69 =	1104	91 =	1456
4 =	64	26 =	416	48 =	768	70 =	1120	92 =	1472
5 =	80	27 =	432	49 =	784	71 =	1136	93 =	1488
6 =	96	28 =	448	50 =	800	72 =	1152	94 =	1504
7 =	112	29 =	464	51 =	816	73 =	1168	95 =	1520
8 =	128	30 =	480	52 =	832	74 =	1184	96 =	1536
9 =	144	31 =	496	53 =	848	75 =	1200	97 =	1552
10 =	160	32 =	512	54 =	864	76 =	1216	98 =	1568
11 =	176	33 =	528	55 =	880	77 =	1232	99 =	1584
12 =	192	34 =	544	56 =	896	78 =	1248	100 =	1600
13 =	208	35 =	560	57 =	912	79 =	1264	200 =	3200
14 =	224	36 =	576	58 =	928	80 =	1280	300 =	4800
15 =	240	37 =	592	59 =	944	81 =	1296	400 =	6400
16 =	256	38 =	608	60 =	960	82 =	1312	500 =	8000
17 =	272	39 =	624	61 =	976	83 =	1328	600 =	9600
18 =	288	40 =	640	62 =	992	84 =	1344	700 =	11200
19 =	304	41 =	656	63 =	1008	85 =	1360	800 =	12800
20 =	320	42 =	672	64 =	1024	86 =	1376	900 =	14400
21 =	336	43 =	688	65 =	1040	87 =	1392	1000 =	16000
22 =	352	44 =	704	66 =	1056	88 =	1408	2000 =	32000

TIME-LAPSE CHART

ONE FRAME EXPOSURE INTERVALS	LENGTH OF SCENE IN SECONDS AT 24 FPS							
	5	10	15	20	25	30	45	60
SECONDS	TIME OF ACTION (HOURS AND MINUTES)							
2	0:04	0:08	0:12	0:16	0:20	0:24	0:36	0:48
3	0:06	0:12	0:18	0:24	0:30	0:36	0:54	1:12
4	0:08	0:16	0:24	0:32	0:40	0:48	1:12	1:36
5	0:10	0:20	0:30	0:40	0:50	1:00	1:30	2:00
6	0:12	0:24	0:36	0:48	1:00	1:12	1:48	2:24
7	0:14	0:28	0:42	0:56	1:10	1:24	2:06	2:48
8	0:16	0:32	0:48	1:04	1:20	1:36	2:24	3:12
9	0:18	0:36	0:54	1:12	1:30	1:48	2:42	3:36
10	0:20	0:40	1:00	1:20	1:40	2:00	3:00	4:00
12	0:24	0:48	1:12	1:36	2:00	2:24	3:36	4:48
14	0:28	0:56	1:24	1:52	2:20	2:48	4:12	5:36
16	0:32	1:04	1:36	2:08	2:40	3:12	4:48	6:24
18	0:36	1:12	1:48	2:24	3:00	3:36	5:24	7:12
20	0:40	1:20	2:00	2:40	3:20	4:00	6:00	8:00
25	0:50	1:40	2:30	3:20	4:10	5:00	7:30	10:00
30	1:00	2:00	3:00	4:00	5:00	6:00	9:00	12:00
35	1:10	2:20	3:30	4:40	5:50	7:00	10:30	14:00
40	1:20	2:40	4:00	5:20	6:40	8:00	12:00	16:00
45	1:30	3:00	4:30	6:00	7:30	9:00	13:30	18:00
50	1:40	3:20	5:00	6:40	8:20	10:00	15:00	20:00
55	1:50	3:40	5:30	7:20	9:10	11:00	16:30	22:00
MINUTES								
1	2:00	4:00	6:00	8:00	10:00	12:00	18:00	24:00
1.5	3:00	6:00	9:00	12:00	15:00	18:00	27:00	36:00
2	4:00	8:00	12:00	16:00	20:00	24:00	36:00	48:00
2.5	5:00	10:00	15:00	20:00	25:00	30:00	45:00	60:00
3	6:00	12:00	18:00	24:00	30:00	36:00	54:00	72:00
3.5	7:00	14:00	21:00	28:00	35:00	42:00	63:00	84:00
4	8:00	16:00	24:00	32:00	40:00	48:00	72:00	96:00
5	10:00	20:00	30:00	40:00	50:00	60:00	90:00	120:00
6	12:00	24:00	36:00	48:00	60:00	72:00	108:00	144:00
7	14:00	28:00	42:00	56:00	70:00	84:00	126:00	168:00
8	16:00	32:00	48:00	64:00	80:00	96:00	144:00	192:00
9	18:00	36:00	54:00	72:00	90:00	108:00	162:00	216:00
10	20:00	40:00	60:00	80:00	100:00	120:00	180:00	240:00
12	24:00	48:00	72:00	96:00	120:00	144:00	216:00	288:00
14	28:00	56:00	84:00	112:00	140:00	168:00	252:00	336:00
16	32:00	64:00	96:00	128:00	160:00	192:00	288:00	384:00
18	36:00	72:00	108:00	144:00	180:00	216:00	324:00	432:00
20	40:00	80:00	120:00	160:00	200:00	240:00	360:00	480:00
22	44:00	88:00	132:00	176:00	220:00	264:00	396:00	528:00
25	50:00	100:00	150:00	200:00	250:00	300:00	450:00	600:00
30	60:00	120:00	180:00	240:00	300:00	360:00	540:00	720:00
35	70:00	140:00	210:00	280:00	350:00	420:00	630:00	840:00
40	80:00	160:00	240:00	320:00	400:00	480:00	720:00	960:00
45	90:00	180:00	270:00	360:00	450:00	540:00	810:00	1080:00
50	100:00	200:00	300:00	400:00	500:00	600:00	900:00	1200:00
55	110:00	220:00	330:00	440:00	550:00	660:00	990:00	1320:00
HOURS								
1	120:00	240:00	360:00	480:00	600:00	720:00	1080:00	1440:00
1.5	180:00	360:00	540:00	720:00	900:00	1080:00	1620:00	2160:00
2	240:00	480:00	720:00	960:00	1200:00	1440:00	2160:00	2880:00
2.5	300:00	600:00	900:00	1200:00	1500:00	1800:00	2700:00	3600:00
3	360:00	720:00	1080:00	1440:00	1800:00	2160:00	3240:00	4320:00

Example: 20 second scene over four hours equals one exposure every 30 seconds.

Hours of Daylight

The size of the sun as seen from earth is 0° 32' 35" or about ½°. The sun moves 15° every hour; 1° every four minutes
In the northern hemisphere, the longest day is June 21, the shortest is December 22. The reverse is true in the south.

Latitude	Jan	Feb	March	April	May	June	July	Aug	Sept	Oct	Nov	Dec
65°N	5.0	8.5	11.8	15.3	18.8	21.9	20.0	16.5	13.0	9.6	6.2	3.6
60°N	6.7	9.2	11.8	14.6	17.2	18.8	18.0	15.6	12.8	10.1	7.5	5.9
55°N	7.8	9.7	11.9	14.2	16.2	17.4	16.8	14.9	12.7	10.5	8.4	7.2
50°N	8.5	10.1	11.9	13.8	15.5	16.4	15.9	14.5	12.6	10.8	9.0	8.1
45°N	9.2	10.4	11.9	13.5	14.9	15.6	15.3	14.0	12.5	11.0	9.5	8.8
40°N	9.7	10.7	12.0	13.3	14.4	15.0	14.7	13.7	12.4	11.2	10.0	9.4
35°N	10.1	10.9	12.0	13.1	14.0	14.5	14.3	13.5	12.4	11.3	10.3	9.8
30°N	10.4	11.1	12.0	12.9	13.7	14.1	13.9	13.2	12.3	11.4	10.6	10.2
25°N	10.8	11.3	12.0	12.8	13.4	13.7	13.5	13.0	12.3	11.6	10.9	10.6
20°N	11.1	11.5	12.0	12.6	13.1	13.3	13.2	12.8	12.3	11.7	11.2	11.0
15°N	11.3	11.7	12.1	12.5	12.8	13.0	12.9	12.6	12.2	11.8	11.4	11.3
10°N	11.6	12.8	12.1	12.4	12.6	12.7	12.6	12.5	12.2	11.9	11.6	11.5
5°N	11.9	12.0	12.1	12.2	12.4	12.4	12.4	12.3	12.1	12.0	11.9	11.8
0°	12.0	12.0	12.1	12.0	12.0	12.0	12.0	12.0	12.1	12.0	12.0	12.0

Hours of Daylight

Latitude	Jan	Feb	March	April	May	June	July	Aug	Sept	Oct	Nov	Dec
5°S	12.4	12.3	12.1	12.0	11.9	11.8	11.9	12.0	12.1	12.2	12.4	12.4
10°S	13.7	12.4	12.2	11.9	11.7	11.6	11.6	11.8	12.0	12.3	12.6	12.7
15°S	12.9	12.6	12.2	11.8	11.4	11.3	11.3	11.6	12.0	12.4	12.8	13.0
20°S	13.2	12.8	12.2	11.6	11.2	10.9	11.0	11.4	12.0	12.6	13.1	13.3
25°S	13.5	12.9	12.2	11.5	10.9	10.6	10.7	11.3	12.0	12.7	13.4	13.7
30°S	13.9	13.1	12.3	11.3	10.6	10.2	10.4	11.1	11.9	12.8	13.7	14.1
35°S	14.3	13.4	12.3	11.2	10.3	9.8	10.0	10.8	11.9	13.0	14.0	14.5
40°S	14.7	13.6	12.3	11.0	9.9	9.3	9.6	10.6	11.9	13.2	14.4	15.0
45°S	15.2	13.9	12.4	10.8	9.5	8.8	9.1	10.3	11.8	13.4	14.8	15.6
50°S	15.9	14.3	12.5	10.5	9.0	8.1	8.5	9.9	11.8	13.6	15.4	16.4
55°S	16.7	14.7	12.5	10.2	8.3	7.2	7.7	9.5	11.7	13.9	16.1	17.3
60°S	18.0	15.3	12.6	9.8	7.4	5.9	6.6	8.9	11.6	14.3	17.1	18.8

Calculations were made for the 15th of each month using sunPATH

"Natural" Lighting For Interior Sets

by Arthur Miller, ASC

With the advent of smaller lighting units, faster film emulsions and digital photography, miniature lighting units have become the fine brushes by which the cinematographer can paint precise light-effects with the small delicate brush-strokes he has long needed. For practical illustrations of some of the methods of using these small lighting units for precision lighting I have turned to specific scenes I have photographed.

Figure A. In lighting this scene there were three paramount considerations. First, we had to make it logical that the face of pseudo monk should remain darkly invisible to the heroine, yet at the same time, when the monk turn during a later phase of action, his face must be visible to the audience. Second, the heroine must be lighted as to present her beauty attractively. Third, the set had to be lit in such a way as to be compositionally attractive, and to make the lighting on the two people believable.

The accompanying diagram shows how this scene was lighted using three 500-Watt Baby Keglights and six 150-watt Dinky Inkies. Baby key #1 provided the key-light. It not only illuminated the heroine, but also provided a logical reason for keeping the monk's face heavily shadowed beneath his cowl. Baby key #7, placed high on the lamp-deck, provided the necessary backlighting on the heroine and on the railing behind her, to separate them from the background. Baby Key #6 also on the overhead lamp-deck, provided additional top-backlight on the set and players from this necessarily important angle.

Dinky Inkies #s 2 and 3 were concealed behind the flowers on the altar in the background, and were directed

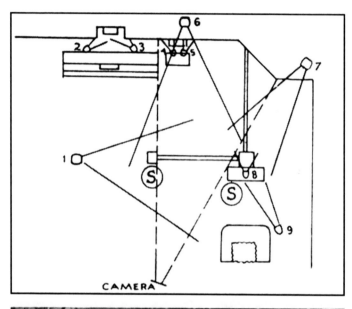

The Mark of Zorro (1940)

Figure A

upward along the wall. It will be noticed that their beams fall in front of the candlesticks at the altar, throwing their shadows against the wall— a logical and necessary effect, since these candles were not lighted. On the other hand, Dinky Inkies #s 4 and 5, which were concealed behind the flowers at the smaller altar, cast their flooded and diffused beams on the wall behind the candlesticks and on the statue. This again is logical, for these beams simulate the natural, visual effect of the light from these lighted candles. These small lamps, which can be concealed so easily within the scene, permit us to get away from the unnatural method of creating such lighted-lamp effects by means of a concentrated beam from a spotlight on the opposite lamp-deck, which inevitably defeats its purpose by also casting on the back-wall the shadow of the light-fixture which is supposed to be producing the illumination! Dinky Inky #8 performs a similar service for the candles before the figure directly behind the heroine, while Dinky Inky #9 completes the lighting by providing a soft "filler-light" in that corner of the set.

Figure B is another candlelight scene. Here, the problem was to provide a convincing effect of candlelight (with a trace of waning daylight outside the window in the left background) and yet provide the necessary illumination for the action—melodramatic swordplay—and to strike the correct visual mood for this type of action.

Again the key light was a 500-Watt Baby Keglight (#1) shining across the table and strongly illuminating the frightened man in the chair. It also served to illuminate part of the back wall behind him, and to throw upon it a pictorially strong shadow of man and chair. Baby Key #2, placed high on the lamp-deck, served a similar purpose for the masked swordsman and created a strong highlight on the white back-wall, against which his dark garments stand out prominently.

The alcove in the background was illuminated by lamp #3—a heavily-diffused Broad—while the effect of

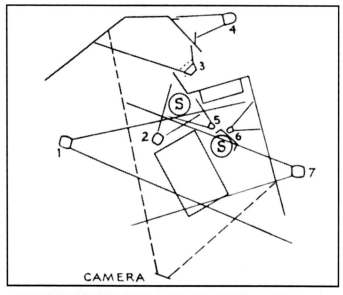

The Mark of Zorro (1940)   Figure B

pale sunlight coming through the window in the background, and projecting its shadow-pattern on the far wall at the left, was produced by a heavily-diffused arc spotlight placed outside the window #4.

It will be obvious that since the swordsman stands leaning against the tall candlestick, the chief illumination on his face and figure should come from that source. It actually came from lamp #5, a Dinky Inky, placed on the floor slightly nearer the camera than the candlestick, and concealed from the lens by the table and chair. Another Inky, #6, with its beam flooded and diffused, completes the lighting by lightening the shadows on the corner behind the players.

In **Figure C**, we have another candlelight effect—this time played in a more somberly dramatic mood. The principal source of illumination appears to be the candle on the table. This was simulated by Dinky Inky # 1, placed on the table, concealed behind the tall hat, which threw its beam strongly up into the face of the actor in the background, and projected his shadow on the back-wall. A second Inky #2, similarly concealed behind the hat, throws its more diffused beam against the other wall, also simulating the candle's light. Inky #3, on the floor at left, continues this effect, and silhouettes the man in the left foreground, #4 a Baby Keglight placed well to the left, outlines the man in the foreground on that side, and aids in lighting the background actor and the wall behind him. Another Baby Keglight #7 on the back lamp deck is crossed to illuminate the two men on the right.

The lighting is completed by the use of two arc spotlights. #5 was used to illuminate the backing outside the window. #6, well flooded, shone through the window to provide rim lighting on the two figures at the right.

Figure D is an example of the simplicity of dramatic effect lighting. The principal source of the light would obviously be the oil lamp suspended over the table.

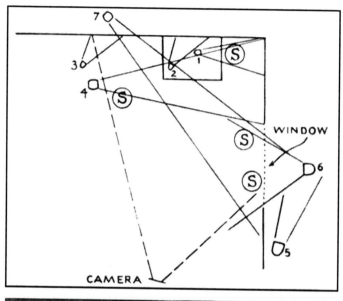

Brigham Young—Frontiersman (1940)

Figure C

This was made the source by placing a Photoflood bulb inside the lampshade at "A" and reinforcing this source with lamp #1, a Baby Keglight placed overhead.

The strong key lighting on the group of three by the left window—especially centering on the distant figure, was provided by lamp #2, an Inky Dinky, placed on the table and concealed from the camera by the man seated in the foreground. The equally strong lighting on the other man seated behind the table was provided by Inky #3, placed on the table in much the same way and concealed from the lens by the man standing in the foreground. Lamp #4—another Inky—gave the rim lighting necessary to make the man standing at the end of the table stand out well from his dark background. Lamp #5, a diffused arc spotlight, provided the effect of faint light coming in through the left-hand window while Broads #'s 6 and 7 illuminated the backing outside the window.

But Dinky Inkies are by no means the only units, which can at times be concealed within the scene. **Figure E** illustrates this. Here we have a stage exterior night-effect. In this the principal light-source is of course the fire. To begin with, two No. 2 Photoflood globes were placed behind the fire; the flickering firelight-effect was created by the usual gadget, which burns an oil-soaked wick in a metal pan directly behind these lamps, so that the smoke interrupts their beams to produce the requisite flicker and variation of intensity.

The chief light-source on the principal players in front of the wagon was a Baby Key, #1, placed low on the ground by the fire, and concealed by the men sitting in the left foreground. Lamp #2, an Inky, similarly placed, illuminated the man standing at the left, while #3, another Inky, highlighted the two men sitting at the left by the fire. Lamp #4 a Baby Keg placed high on the lamp-deck, at the rear left, was used to rim-light the players at the left and center-foreground. Extremely soft front lighting was

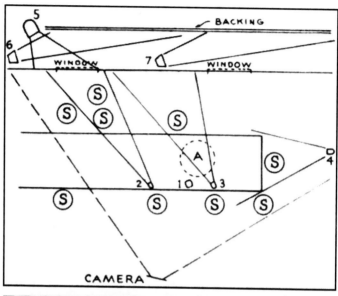

Brigham Young—Frontiersman (1940)

Figure D

provided by lamp #5—a heavily diffused Broad.

The background was highlighted by lamp #6, a Baby Keg placed high at the right and crossed, while the backing was illuminated by #7, another diffused Broad.

The point which I hope these somewhat obvious examples discussed will make is this: That these natural source-lighting effects, together with many similar ones they suggest, would have been absolutely impossible previous to the introduction of today's high-speed emulsions and less powerful lamp-units that the speed of these films have made possible.

Cinematographers have always looked forward to the day when they could get truly natural light-effects, and work at substantially natural levels of illumination. Today, thanks to these modern technical developments, we have come incredibly close to being able to achieve this long-sought goal. While average interior light-levels are of course subject to considerable variation, due to differences in the methods of individual directors of photography and to the processing standards of the different laboratories which handle their film, a surprising majority of cinematographers are working only slightly above normal practical room-lighting levels

It should be pointed out also that this remarkable development has had, in addition to its artistic benefits, very definite technical and economic advantages as well. By eliminating the need for high illumination levels and the larger and bulkier lamps necessary for many of the makeshift techniques formerly needed to make these larger lamps adaptable to the fine, precision lighting these effects demand.

Summing the matter up. Today's cinematographers are most fortunate that we can today reap the benefits of these advances in film, lenses and lighting equipment, which on the one hand make it possible at last to light with the precision necessary to obtain really natural light-

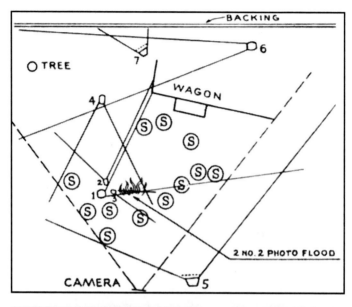

Brigham Young—Frontiersman (1940)

Figure E

ing effects, and on the other, to greatly simplify and expedite the work of director of photography and his stage crew.

Editor's Note: *The introduction of small incandescent lighting units in the 1940s, the Tungsten-Halogen revolution of the 1960s, the HMI daylight balanced units of the 1970s and today's development of miniature LED units constitute a significant step forward in the technology of motion picture lighting. All of this coupled with the digital capture we now have, have made a genuine breakthrough in the art and craft of cinematography.*

A clarification of lighting unit terms used by Mr. Miller:

Baby Keglight: *also called Baby or Keg (because of the barrel like shape of the fixture). A 6" Fresnel spotlight using 500, 750 or 1000 watt globes.*

Dinky Inky: *Also called Inky Dink or Inky (denotes smallest incandescent). A 3" or smaller Fresnel spotlight using 50, 75, 100, 150 or 200 watt globes.*

Broad: *Also called a Broadside, single Broad (one globe) or double Broad (two globes). A flood type unit, rectangular in shape with Factorlite glass in front. Uses 500, 750, 1000 or 1500 watt globes.*

Excerpted from *Charles Clarke's Professional Cinematography* (1968) originally from an article in *American Cinematographer*, September 1966

Recommended Reading

Biographies and Interviews

Laszlo, ASC, Andrew, *It's A Wrap!,* Hollywood, CA; ASC Press, 2004.

Walker, ASC, Joseph, *The Light On Her Face,* Hollywood, CA; ASC Press, 1984.

Zone, Ray (editor), *New Wave King: The Cinematography of Laszlo Kovacs, ASC,* Hollywood, CA, ASC Press, 2002.

Zone, Ray (editor), *Writer of Light: The Cinematography of Vittorio Storaro, ASC, AIC,* Hollywood, CA, ASC Press, 2001.

Cinematography

Burum, ASC, Stephen H. (editor), *American Cinematographer Manual*–9th edition, Hollywood, CA, ASC Press, 2004.

Clarke, ASC, Charles G., *Professional Cinematography,* Hollywood, CA, ASC Press, 2002.

Groticelli, Michael (editor), *American Cinematographer Video Manual,* Hollywood, CA, ASC Press, 2002.

Wilson, Anton, *Anton Wilson's Cinema Workshop,* Hollywood, CA; ASC Press, 1983, 1994.

Color

Eastman Kodak Publication H-12, *An Introduction to Color,* Rochester, 1972.

Eastman Kodak Publication E-74, *Color As Seen and Photographed,* Rochester, 1972.

Eastman Kodak Publication H-188, *Exploring the Color Image,* Rochester.

Film

Eastman Kodak Publication H-1: Eastman Professional Motion Picture Films.

Eastman Kodak Publication H-23: The Book of Film Care.

Eastman Kodak Publication H-740: Basic Photographic Sensitometry Workbook.

Eastman Kodak Publication N-17: Infrared Films.

Eastman Kodak Publication: ISO vs EI Speed Ratings.

Eastman Kodak Publication T8-133: Cine Exposure Calculator.

Eastman Kodak Publication: Ultraviolet and Fluorescence Photography.

Film History

Turner, George E., *The Cinema of Adventure, Romance and Terror,* Hollywood, CA; ASC Press, 1989.

Film Processing

Eastman Kodak publications: H-1, H-2, H-7, H-17, H-21, H-23, H-24.07, H-26, H-36, H-37, H-37A, H-44, H-61, H-61A, H-61B, H-61C, H-61D, H-61E, H-61F, H-807 and H-822.

Filters

Eastman Kodak Publication B-3: Filters.

Eastman Kodak Publication KW-13: Filter Workbook.

Hirschfeld, ASC, Gerald, *Image Control,* Hollywood, CA; ASC Press, 2005.

Journals and Magazines

American Cinematographer, ASC Holding Corp.,www.theasc.com.

SMPTE Journal, Society of Motion Picture and Television Engineers,www.smpte.org.

Lighting

Bergery, Benjamin, *Reflections - 21 Cinematographers at Work,* Hollywood, CA; ASC Press, 2002.

Visual Effects

Abbott, ASC, L.B., *Special Effects with Wire, Tape and Rubber Bands,* Hollywood, CA; ASC Press, 1984.

Dunn, ASC, Linwood, and Turner, George E., *ASC Treasury of Visual Effects,* Hollywood, CA; ASC Press,1983.

Notes:

Notes:

Notes:

CPSIA information can be obtained at www.ICGtesting.com
Printed in the USA
LVOW120710250612

287453LV00001B/7/P